So when Evita and Anabella, the miniature horses, came on heat again we knew what we were required to do. We got Piccolo comfortably dossed down in his own lust-hatch, an airy stable with plenty of hay and oats to keep up his amorous energies. Every three or four hours we would bring in one of the mares and help Piccolo do his stuff exactly as we had been instructed. This went on for two days. I don't know whether the pace was killing for Piccolo but it certainly was for us.

By the third morning I was completely shattered. It was then I committed a terrible *faux pas*. I didn't feel strong enough to walk across the walled garden so I called over to John, 'Darling, let's go and mate again. It's at least three hours since we did it last.'

Rosamund Fisher

My Jungle Babies

Arrow Books

Arrow Books Limited
3 Fitzroy Square, London W1P 6JD

An imprint of the Hutchinson Publishing Group

London Melbourne Sydney Auckland
Wellington Johannesburg and agencies
throughout the world

First published by Allen & Unwin 1979
Arrow edition 1981
© Rosamund Fisher 1979

Made and printed in Great Britain
by The Anchor Press Ltd
Tiptree, Essex

ISBN 0 09 926000 X

Contents

1. Amazons in Norfolk   1
2. Charlie the Stowaway   16
3. Feeding a Family on Steak Tartare   32
4. Panama and Spider Monkeys   46
5. Sex with the Miniature Horses   59
6. By Paddle down the Amazon   66
7. Monkey Business   75
8. The Plague of Giant Rats   94
9. Rudolf and Mrs Wolf   107
10. Camels of the Incas   114
11. Ellie Ocelot and Others   123
12. Jubilee the Jaguar   130
13. An Argentinian Shark   137
14. The First Falabellas   147
15. Adventures of a Norfolk Vet   159
16. The Falabellas Meet the Queen   167

To John
with my love

I

Amazons in Norfolk

If the urge should take you to open a Latin American zoo in Norfolk, peopled with weird and wonderful tropical creatures that no vet in the country has ever heard of, what better day to do it than April Fool's Day? And come to think of it, who better to present the mad enterprise to the public than a comedian?

'You must be joking,' stammered Frank Muir when we sprang the idea on him, unfairly, after a very good dinner. Frank's wife, Polly, and I have been close friends since we were about ten years old. Short of a multiple fracture, Frank knew there was no way of getting out of it.

He dutifully turned up, complete with pink bow tie, Polly, their son Jamie and daughter Sally, at Kilverstone on the eve of 1 April 1973. The state of the place made it a little hard to believe that we really intended to open the following day. The animals had been settled down comfortably enough in their cages, and the flamingos and macaws could boast their own walled gardens among the lawns and meadows that slope gently down towards the river Thet.

But the visitors were not quite so well off. There were big bald patches in the lawns where turf had still to be laid; signs still to be put up; buildings unfinished. April Fool's Day had actually taken us by surprise. My husband, John, had been hounded by the press and television for months after they had got wind of the news that the third Baron Fisher of Kilverstone planned to turn his estate into a home for strange beasts with names like capybaras, coatimundis and agoutis. They sensed a good story and kept pressing him to name the opening date. John finally weakened and said 1 April – the first date that sprang into his head. We found ourselves stuck with it.

'Poor darlings,' Frank groaned, 'you've got British builders. I can't think what the public are going to say about your loos.'

The builders had indeed let us down. They had only got as far as the scaffolding for the sewage works, but their real triumph was the ladies' loos. You walked in the door and saw a row of eight loos, positioned indecently side by side along one wall without a single partition between them.

'What are you going to do with them?' Frank chortled. 'Is milady going to sit there and encourage the old dears? What happens if the vicar's wife walks in?'

It doesn't pay to be over-funny. I got my own back by conscripting all the Muirs to help us in a last-minute attempt to finish off the new lawns. The turf had arrived in neat green squares two weeks before. But we had been so busy finishing the animal cages, the shop and the cafeteria, slaving away by night under floodlights, that we had not had time to lay all of it. In the March drizzle, it was not long before our ready-made lawn turned into slimy yellow matting with worms sticking out all over it. We spread this unappealing stuff hopefully over the bare earth beside the monkey house and clumped up and down, up and down, in our wellingtons, trying to make the grass look as if it had been sprouting for ever.

'You know,' said Frank, 'this reminds me of the Irishman who saw a load of turf like this going past on a lorry and called out, "I wish I was rich enough to have my grass sent away to be cut."'

Cecil, the woolly monkey, glowered at Frank from behind the wire of his cage, obviously unamused.

By breakfast on opening day, the culmination of nine months of planning and working, often late into the night by floodlight, we were exhausted. We had two baby badgers living in the house, which would snuffle along at my heels, one behind the other, exactly as they would follow their real mother. Before our guests got their breakfast, the baby badgers had to be given their big bottles of powdered milk.

'I smell rain,' said Frank Muir, with a rasher of bacon hanging from his fork. 'It could even be snow. I do hope someone will come.'

Anyone who has had to organise a meeting knows that butterflies-in-the-stomach feeling that comes as the clock ticks away and you start to wonder whether anyone is going to arrive. Had we sent out enough invitations? Would a Latin American zoo really catch the fancy of the public? Since some drab little pen-pusher in the local council had stopped us from putting up signs on the main road, would visitors even be able to find Kilverstone?

We need not have worried. Come mid-morning, the cars were standing bumper-to-bumper both ways down the A11, which runs just outside the entrance to the park.

Our collection of animals was fairly modest in those days, but it contained many creatures that are rarely seen in Britain, and still less in Norfolk. There were the camel's woolly South American cousins, llamas, alpacas and guanacos; we had chosen a splendid alpaca called Chocolate Drop, with luxuriant black curls and drooping eyelashes that would have made any girl envious, to be the symbol of our zoo. We had brightly-plumed macaws and toucans, birds that sounded like a tinkling waterfall, black-masked raccoons and snuffly peccaries, grumpy woolly monkeys, precocious white-fronted capuchins and shy little green-headed squirrel monkeys. And our first residents seemed determined to make their presence felt.

Chocolate Drop, the alpaca, decided to break out of his enclosure and inspect our visitors and their strange machines.

3

He set off on a stately trot around the car park in the company of Juan, the guanaco.

'Ooh, I didn't know Kilverstone was a *safari* park,' exclaimed one tweedy visitor as Juan and Chocolate Drop bore down upon him. But when Juan fixed him with a large, liquid eye and displayed a fine set of molars, he beat a cautious retreat to the cafeteria. All the llama family can deliver memorable bites and like their cousins, the camels, they are proficient spitters as well. Happily for all, Chocolate Drop and Juan were in a good mood on opening day. Having concluded that the visitors' cars were inoffensive, they allowed the keepers to lead them back to their paddocks.

Frank made a funny speech and released half a dozen free-flying budgerigars from a basket. Afterwards, I strolled about the park with my sister, Mary, to see how the visitors were enjoying the animals – and what the animals were making of them! Mary had driven up specially from her home in Berkshire. She has a delicious sense of fun. When I showed her the ladies' loos and told her what Frank had suggested, she snorted with laughter.

'Oh yes,' she said. 'Do let's sit down and watch the faces of the first people who come in. We'll only pretend. Come on, I dare you.'

'Well, I might if you go first.'

'No, both together. Ready? One, two, three!'

As we both bobbed down, two very large and sober matrons with a howling mite in tow sailed through the door.

'Well I never,' said one. The other silently goggled at us as we hurriedly rose to our feet.

'Come along, Maud,' ordered the first lady. They began to march out together, a picture of indignation, but the child howled louder than before, 'Mummy, I can't wait.'

We were the ones who were red-faced as we slunk out.

Setting up a zoo, of course, is no joke. But anyone who is tempted to have a try should be forewarned that a good sense of humour is one of the absolute conditions for survival.

Some people imagine that having a private zoo must be rather a luxury, like keeping polo ponies or a collection of vintage cars. I suppose it is rather a luxury to live surrounded by the endless fascination of wild animals from the other side of the world. But the price is fairly steep. You have to be prepared, to begin with, to work a basic twelve-hour day and to double up, whenever required, as amateur vet, do-it-yourself builder, foster-mother, dog-catcher, dish-washer and ticket-seller.

Having animals in the family has meant getting up every three hours throughout the night to bottle-feed baby monkeys, jaguars and raccoons, prowling about in the small hours in pursuit of a runaway capybara or spider monkey, and helping the miniature horses to mate. It has amounted to a non-stop crash course in zoology – reading every book I could lay my hands on, pumping the experts at other zoos and above all learning from the animals themselves, both at Kilverstone and in the wilds of Central and South America.

John has had to put up with monkey business in his bed night after night. But zoo-keeping for him has also meant endless financial headaches and endless dealings with bank managers, accountants, local authorities, caterers, animal dealers, embassies and airlines. A zoo is business as well as pleasure. Anyone who has ever tried to run one knows that it is very hard to make ends meet, let alone produce a profit – which is why nearly all the big zoos around the world are paid for by the taxpayer.

We are often asked: why on earth did you decide to do it? It is a question people are bound to ask. There we were in middle life, with no obvious qualifications for zoo-keeping and more romantic notions than practical knowledge about Latin America and its wildlife.

But some ambitions are born young. When I was a very plain little girl with freckles, my strapping elder brother, Hugh, sat me down on a log in the park at Ugbrooke, the family home in Devon, and gave me a lecture.

'Rosamund,' he said sternly, 'you must never, never become a film star. That would be letting the family down.'

Hugh had somehow got it into his head that this, sooner or later, was what I would set my sights on.

'But Hugh,' I protested, 'I don't want to be a film star.'

'Well, what *do* you want to be then?' Hugh, who had solemnly made up his mind to go into the Army (and later did) had no patience with anyone whose plans were less definite.

'I want to keep animals, lots and lots of animals. I'd like to have a kennel and breed dogs. Or a riding school, with masses of horses.'

Hugh harrumphed. 'Uncle won't stand for any of that, Bubbles.'

And indeed Uncle didn't. My mother had died when I was a baby and, since my father was constantly travelling around the world, Hugh and I and our sister, Mary, were entrusted to my uncle's care at Ugbrooke, the seat of the Clifford family in Devon. My uncle was kind to us in many ways but would not stand for animals around the house. I was not even allowed to keep a puppy.

'Messy things,' Uncle would growl. 'Someone brought a dog into the house once and it crawled right into my bed. When I went to sleep that night, I put my foot right into the mess it had made.'

As I couldn't have a puppy, I collected every other living creature I could. I had pet snails, but they are pretty dreary things and it was difficult to talk them into having races with each other. My first real pet was a call duck that was given to me by one of the keepers at Ugbrooke. The call duck is a white cousin of the mallard, and its role during a shoot was supposed to be to lead other birds across the guns.

I called mine Dilly and he went everywhere with me. I taught him to swim as best I could in an old hip-bath that I found in an attic. I also took him into my own bath with me but he didn't care much for warm water. Dilly met a sad end some months later: he wandered from the house into the park and was eaten by a fox.

I strolled forlornly around the Ugbrooke estate for weeks afterwards, imagining how its lakes and streams would look if Uncle could be persuaded to make them a home for penguins, seals and otters. He would hear nothing of it. The three lakes at Ugbrooke were full of trout and the men of the family – all keen fishermen – had no intention of turning them over to a small girl's fancies.

On every trip to London I would demand to be taken to the Zoo. Years later, when I had children of my own, I went exploring in the pet department of Harrods and fell in love with a baby chimpanzee called Sam. I resolved to buy him as a playmate for my youngest child, Charles, who was then only six months old. I was sure they would both fit comfortably into the pram, and Sam was so precocious that I thought he might teach Charles a thing or two. I was only deterred when Charles's nanny, a placid, even-tempered lady with a heart of gold, dug her heels in. 'I'm not going to face the other nannies in the park with that thing, ma'am. It's the chimp or me.'

I was thwarted again. But my childhood ambition to rear animals stayed with me. It never occurred to me that, instead of a pet, I would end up with an entire zoo!

John did not entirely share my obsession with animals – at least, not at the beginning. He still tells stories against himself about his early fear of dogs and horses, which lasted right up until his student days at Cambridge, when he lived in terror of his landlady's snappish Pekinese. I am sure that before we married, each of us for the second time, in 1970 he had never dreamed that he would one day become a zoo-keeper.

It was not long before the subject of animals came up. John had been wondering how to make better use of a hundred acres or so of the Kilverstone estate, between the house, the Norman church with its round tower, and the river Thet. It was a delightful stretch of walled garden and water meadows where John's father had planted some 1,500 fruit trees which he delighted in pruning himself after he retired from the Indian Civil Service.

John had been depressed by the steady advance of the asphalt and redbrick housing estates of Thetford over this corner of Norfolk countryside, which is exceptionally rich in history as well as beauty. A Saxon road ran through the Kilverstone lands, with a Roman settlement on the brow of the hill and a medieval village just beyond the church. A few miles away, at Snarehill, is the battlefield where King Edmund of East Anglia made his last-ditch stand against the Danes. He lost. The Danes ceremoniously shot him full of arrows and the people of the area were forced to pay Danegeld of seven pence a year. You cannot dig deeply anywhere on the Kilverstone estate without turning up ancient drains or the remains of medieval buildings.

The original house was built in the reign of James I on the site of Monk's Hall Manor by Thomas Wright, whose descendant became the famous Governor of Georgia: Governor Wright was the last Royal Governor before and during the War of Independence, but was so admired by the people of Georgia that he was asked to resume the post as first Republican Governor. The estate stayed in the same family until it was bought in 1895 by an energetic and far-sighted arms manufacturer called Josiah Vavasseur, who was the director of a big gun and shipbuilding company based at Newcastle upon Tyne. Vavasseur was one of the pioneers of modern naval weaponry. He created a device that could absorb the energy of recoil of a gun and permit lighter and simpler gun mountings to be used on fighting ships. His business brought him into contact with John's grandfather, 'Jacky' Fisher, then rising fast in a meteoric career that was to make him not only Admiral of the Fleet but the most famous British seaman since Nelson, justly revered as the founder of the modern British Navy.

They met often around the turn of the century to discuss plans for modernising the navy and the Fishers were often invited up to shoot at Kilverstone. Josiah Vavasseur, who was childless, took a great liking to Jacky Fisher's son, Cecil. When Vavasseur died in 1907, he left Kilverstone to Cecil on the sole condition that he and his heirs should use the name Vavasseur as a middle name.

Kilverstone was a place of peace and solace for the Admiral of the Fleet during his stormy battles with his rivals in the Navy and his enemies in Parliament. Jacky Fisher often stayed at Kilverstone in the years before his death in 1920, using his son's estate as his own country seat. He loved the old house with its stone walls and gabled roofs, its curlicued clock-tower and its great walled gardens. He was often to be found before breakfast tramping up and down a grass path, bordered with yews, that soon became known as the 'Admiral's Walk'. King Edward VII came to visit Jacky Fisher at Kilverstone in 1909; 'it was sweet of him', the Admiral commented in a letter to a friend.

Kilverstone Hall is still full of papers and mementoes of Jack Fisher – the billiards room is lined with original cartoons and caricatures of him in many famous scrapes, of both the political and the military sort. But the memento of Jacky Fisher that no visitor to the park can fail to miss stands on the eastern side of the flamingo pool, beside the 'Admiral's Walk' of which he was so fond. It is the brilliantly coloured figurehead from HMS *Calcutta*, the ship on which Jacky Fisher put to sea as a midshipman to join the British fleet blockading the Baltic Sea in 1854 in support of the Crimean operation.

The figurehead presents the turbaned, jewelled and richly moustachioed image of an Indian potentate with the improbable name of Sir Jamset Jeegigiboy, a great friend of the British Raj. A highly respected Parsee baronet, Sir Jamset had presented HMS *Calcutta*, one of a class of four ships built in Bombay, to Queen Victoria. His figurehead is

9

believed to be the largest that survives, and probably the largest ever built. Although time and weather have taken their toll of the teak wood from which it was carved, it has been perfectly restored. John's father managed to get permission from the Admiralty to buy it and move it to Kilverstone in 1922.

This was the setting for our zoo: not the sort of place where you would immediately expect to find birds and animals from the Amazon jungle, the high Andes or the Argentine pampas. But why not?

At the time we married, John had been farming for the best part of twenty years. He is no fanatical conservationist, but he is appalled to see the destruction of some of the prettiest parts of the countryside and to see how people living in towns are more and more cut off from their roots. It seems that fewer and fewer people have the chance to learn what the countryside means. People who live in big cities are not living any more naturally than the animals in London Zoo – probably less so. They are cooped up in an artificial environment from which nature is almost completely excluded. Is an animal cage as cruel as a high-rise block of flats for city children?

'When you think about it,' John said one night, 'England was pretty much a free-range country before the Enclosure Acts. But how many people today can actually sit down beside a stream that isn't full of poisonous chemicals and watch birds and animals ranging about?'

John wanted to find a way to open part of Kilverstone, and particularly the long, shady river walk, to the public. He was thinking at this stage about setting up some kind of general recreation park, but found little support from the local authorities or the Countryside Commission.

The idea of starting a zoo seized both of us at once during a visit to an old friend in the west country who had set up a wildlife park from scratch, with little preparation beyond a lifelong passion for all living things. We should have been warned off, I suppose, by his trials and tribulations. But what made a strong impression on us was the way he had used a walled garden as part of the setting for his zoo, so that the landscape was not scarred by those hideous concrete jungles that are put up in so many zoos by architects who seem to be more concerned with their own drawing-board fantasies than with the needs of the animals and the appearance of the whole thing. Zoos do not have to be ugly.

There are people who say that it is cruel to keep animals in cages. It certainly can be, if you treat animals purely as exhibits and deny them the privacy, the diversions and the sense of territorial possession that they need. But I do not accept for one moment that animals are necessarily any happier in the wild than in captivity, if their owners are sensitive to their basic needs.

Even the boredom that animals are said to suffer in a zoo is often exaggerated. You can be bored anywhere. Animals mark out a 'territory' for themselves and, wherever they are, their lives are very much circumscribed by this sense of territory. In the case of some of the smaller creatures that make their homes in the middle levels of the rainforest, this 'territory' may be no bigger than a few branches, an area smaller than the cage to which it is transplanted. Sloths are known to have spent more than a year on a single bough. And in zoos, animals have a new source of diversion: the human beings who display a curious variety of facial expressions and 'ooh ah' noises on the other side of the cage. Many animals, especially monkeys, enjoy being near people. They keep *us* under observation too.

There is one kind of excitement that animals do not get in zoos. Unless the zoo keepers are dangerously incompetent, zoo animals are rarely engaged in stalking and eating each other. Most people who talk of the supposed cruelty of zoos are sublimely unaware of the cruelty of nature. In the jungle, most species are engaged in a life-or-death struggle, the war of all against all. In their native habitat, our capuchins or capybaras would make a tasty snack for Jason, our jaguar.

Where man has not intruded on nature, an ecological balance has been established that will ensure the survival of most species, but life is still very precarious for any creature that could make a meal for a predator. Man, of course, is the greatest predator of all, and wherever man has intruded on the wild with his guns, his traps, his pesticides and his diseases, the survival of whole species is imperilled. The more we can learn about the endangered species, the more successful our efforts to breed them in captivity, the more likely they are to survive.

Zoos are for people, too. We had an ideal natural setting at Kilverstone, in a river valley that had been the home of Romans, Saxons and Normans, where the birds and animals could be displayed amongst flower beds and blossoming trees. We could blend the new buildings with the old, and we decided that wherever possible we would convert old stables and farm buildings so as to preserve the architectural style of the estate. We turned a large greenhouse into a walk-through tropical aviary, a saw shed into a café, an old barn into a shop, and a pig sty and a bull pen into the ladies' and gents' loos respectively.

But we had first to decide on the theme of the zoo. A small private park cannot house as many different animals as the London or Zurich zoos. We didn't have enough space to become a safari park, and in any case, we didn't like the impersonal aspect of those safari parks where you bump along in your car with someone else driving hot on your tail behind, unable to get close enough or linger long enough to really get to know the animals. For me, the real enchantment of a zoo is to be able to dally, sometimes for hours, with animals that you like. This is a very personal thing. After a few visits to zoos, there is nothing very exciting about being dragged from the lions and tigers to the elephants and giraffes and on to the monkeys and the penguins. We wanted to make Kilverstone tantalising, not overwhelming, for our visitors. We wanted to give them a breath of fresh air, away from the strains of city life, to get them out of their cars and tempt them to go to see what is round the next corner, and the next.

After visiting lots of zoos, wildlife parks, bird gardens and safari parks, we realised that we should specialise. That way, we could not only preserve the unique environment of Kilverstone but offer a unique collection of animals which we could breed and which would become the subject for serious study as well as pure enjoyment. So we decided to make Kilverstone the first Latin American zoo in Europe.

Why choose Latin America? It was partly the attraction of the unknown. Latin America had exercised a romantic spell over me since my childhood – a spell that was largely derived from girlish images of Aztec ruins, sun-drenched haciendas and the dizzying carnival season in Rio. Before we conceived the idea of the wildlife park, John and I had travelled less in Latin America than in any other continent. But the dramatic reality of Latin America and its wildlife, which we would encounter on trips in search of new animals, far surpassed the romantic impressions with which I started.

I had only imagined the spectacular natural contrasts of this continent of rainforests and snow-capped mountains, rolling pampas and dead men's deserts. Cut off from the rest of the world until the Isthmus of Panama emerged from the ocean, linking the continent to regions farther north, South America has evolved a variety of birds and animals to match the variety of its landscape. Some ethnologists have described the animals of this New World, taken all together, as the strangest on earth. Many of the species have made remarkable adaptations to remarkable environments, especially in the heart of the Amazonian jungle, where many different sorts of animals have mastered the art of hanging from the branches by their tails, like the spider monkey, the kinkajou and the porcupine, or of swimming and climbing trees, like the jaguar.

No other part of the world can rival the brilliant array of colours of the birds of South America. More than a third of the world's bird species are to be found in the countries between the Rio Grande and the frozen tip of Patagonia, and the dazzling contrasts of plumage within a single family of birds – like the toucans or the macaws – make you feel that an imaginative child has run riot with his paint-box. You can find green-billed, black-billed, red-billed, and yellow-billed toucans, and all sorts of mixes between them: blue-breasted, saffron-breasted, white-, sulphur-, and orange-breasted.

For me the toucan, the 'clown of the forest', hopping from bough to bough, croaking and chattering incessantly through its huge, brightly coloured beak, looking out on the world through a humorous, cynical eye, is one of the joys of the South American rainforest: a symbol of its strangeness and its beauty with which any child (or any child at heart) can identify.

Yet the spectacular variety of Latin American wildlife is rarely seen in its native habitat. The birds and animals conceal themselves high up in the jungle canopy and few attempts have been made to establish modern zoos where people can visit them, or reserves where the survival of imperilled species like the maned wolf, the giant otter or the jaguar can be guaranteed. The cascading variety of colour and sound of the South American rainforest has no rival in Africa or Asia, yet most people – even in the wilds of Brazil or Peru – see these creatures only in photographs and never hear their incredible cries.

This is what gave us our real incentive to start a Latin American zoo. We weren't interested in offering a random collection of animals from all over the world, introduced to the public without feeling for their native environment. Anyway, we thought, most people in Britain have seen a giraffe or an elephant. But how many had even heard of a capybara or a maned wolf or an ora pendola?

At Kilverstone, we hoped to open up a whole New World to our visitors. And in doing that, we hoped to make our own small contribution to the conservation of some of the species of birds and animals that man has endangered through his needless destruction of nature, even in a continent where the wilds seem boundless. Since the arrival of the conquistadores, the animals of South America have been hunted for their meat, their skins or their wool, or slaughtered by farmers as vermin. The rainforests recede under the chain-saws and bulldozers, and their inhabitants are driven back into less hospitable areas. Yet we were told, when we started to plan Kilverstone, that the World Wildlife Fund devoted less than five per cent of its budget to the fauna of South America, which makes it the Cinderella among the world's major wildlife regions. That was a measure of the challenge before us.

2

Charlie the Stowaway

I met the first monkey in the family in the headwaters of the Amazon, in the tropical rainforests of Peru. It was the first expedition that John and I had made together to South America in search of animals. We were staying in a little town called Iquitos, a relic from the days of the rubber boom, whose crowning glory is an ornate edifice, built entirely of cast iron by the man who put up the Eiffel Tower, which had caught the fancy of some Amazonian millionaire and been transplanted to the tropics. In Iquitos we hired a native canoe with an outboard motor and set off downstream to look for animals in the jungle down towards the borders of Brazil.

It was a bumpy ride: the river raced along, whirling great clumps of loose vegetation and fallen boughs along with the current, while our Indian guide zigzagged through them like someone driving a dodgem car. We had to stop from time to time to disentangle vines and leaves from the propeller. On either side of the Amazon, which is less than a mile wide at this stage, the great trees of the rainforest towered for 200 feet or more, alive with the chattering and trilling of animals and birds that remained invisible. The damp heat felt like a Turkish bath.

After fifteen miles or so we reached a jetty. Beyond was a

clearing with two big thatched huts raised up on stilts and almost completely enveloped in chicken-wire and mosquito netting. This was our hotel for the night, which the proprietor proudly identified as the 'Amazon Lodge'. One of the huts was a communal mess, where we dined that night on grilled peccary, sliced up into tiny strips like matchsticks. It had little taste, but cracked with the first bite, and became more and more like leather with every chew. The other hut, also palm-thatched with a wide verandah, was divided up into little cubicles with hammocks, and when the time came to go to bed we were given candles to find the way.

The next morning, we set off down a jungle trail with our guide to rendezvous with a tribe of Indians who range through the forests of Brazil, Peru and Ecuador with superior disdain for such formalities as passports and international frontiers. On this walk through the forest, I heard for the first time the haunting call of the ora pendola. The ora pendola is a large bird looking rather like a crow with a yellow tail. The remarkable thing about it is its call, which starts with a hiss like escaping gas, then becomes a long silvery rattle, broadens out into a rush of music like a stick pulled swiftly over a xylophone and ends in a deep, gong-like sound. But, apart from the occasional flash of a macaw, the creatures of the forest were still invisible to us; the jungle canopy hung far above our heads, blotting out the sky and submerging us in a green dusk.

After much slithering over fallen trees and sling bridges bound together with vines, we reached a lagoon and, on its farther shore, the Indians. We paddled across to them in another canoe. They were brightly got up in head-dresses fashioned from scarlet, blue and yellow macaw feathers, shaped rather like the toque Queen Mary used to wear, with a marmoset tail hanging down behind. They were bare to the waist, wearing a sort of tea-towel below, and bearing immensely long blowpipes which we found they could use with deadly accuracy. They demonstrated their marksmanship by asking us to fold a banknote to the size of a postage stamp and pin it to a post standing in the clearing. From twenty yards away, they took it in turns to aim and fire at this small target. Every one hit it – although some needed two or three tries.

I noticed that one of the Indian women had two tiny brown baby monkeys – marmosets or tamarins – rooting about in her rather greasy black hair. They seemed perfectly at home there, emitting a remarkable variety of bird-like noises.

'Oh, can I touch them?' I asked the guide.

He interpreted, but the woman shook her head firmly.

'She says that they've just been captured,' he explained. 'They're not used to humans, and they would bite you. Anyway, they may be missing their parents. They were last night's dinner.'

The common practice, it seemed, was to net an entire family, put mother and father into the cooking pot at once, and keep the babies until they were big enough to make a decent meal too. In the meantime, the little ones had their uses about the home; they set about with relish digging lice, fleas and flakes of loose skin out of the hair of their captors.

The Indians came up one by one to offer us various animals they had snared in the forest, mostly sloths, capybaras and wild birds. Then one man appeared with another baby monkey peeping out from behind his feathers. It was slightly longer than the others, and turned out to be a red-mantled tamarin. Its head was no bigger than a golf ball but out of it flashed two strikingly intelligent eyes, brimming over with curiosity. The white stripe below its nose looked like a grizzled, close-cropped moustache. It twittered and chirruped and chattered away without pause, obviously bent on explaining its whole view of the world to me.

I fell in love with it at once.

'John,' I said, 'we can't let this baby go into the cooking-pot.'

'You never know, it might taste rather good.' Of course, he wasn't serious. He did, however, make some show of haggling.

After much discussion via the interpreter, we finally arranged the transfer of the tamarin from the Indian's head to mine for the princely sum of four dollars.

'Do let's look at that tree before we go.' John pointed to an enormous tree with huge buttress-roots, taller than either of us, fanning out from the trunk with thick vines hanging down like twisted rope from its lofty boughs.

'There you are,' I said to John, 'that's the sort of thing that Tarzan swings about on.' I grabbed hold of a promising-looking vine and handed it to him.

The tamarin trilled its appreciation as John swung back and forth in a creditable imitation of Johnny Weissmuller. The trouble was that there was a great temptation to let go as the vine swung back towards the base of the tree – which is exactly what John did, not noticing that it was buried in deep mud. As he sank with a great plop up to his thighs in stinking black mud, the tamarin let out a great squeal of delight.

'The trouble with that bloody thing,' said John, 'is it's too human.'

'In that case, we'd better give him a name at once. Or is it a her?'

I appealed to the guide to solve our problem. It is not very easy to be sure of the sex of something as tiny as our new acquisition.

Our guide was philosophical about the problem. 'Call it Charlie,' he said. 'You'll find out in the end.'

So Charlie it was. Not until we got back to England did I realise that Charlie was in fact a girl, and I still find it hard to break the habit of calling her a him.

With Charlie on her new perch, we bumped and splashed our way back upriver to Iquitos, where we soon had to fight off a queue of people trying to sell us various animals under the dire threat that they would otherwise be eaten. I have no doubt that this was indeed so; I also suspect our guide had tipped off some of his neighbours that we were unusually squeamish about what goes into the cooking pot. Our major problem was that the Peruvian government imposes severe restrictions on the traffic in wildlife, which is commendable in principle but not always in practice – for example, not if an animal is going to be eaten if it cannot be exported!

I could not resist one Indian who came trudging into the lobby of our hotel with a sack over his shoulder. He tapped John and pointed at it. I peeped inside and could not see anything in the gloom except a small basket at the bottom. 'Su madre es muerta,' he said. 'Its mother is dead.'

That was enough for me. 'Darling, we just have to have it. It's an orphan.'

'We'd better at least see what it is.'

So the basket was brought out of the sack, and we found inside a superb baby ocelot – exactly what we had most wanted. It was a male and I called him Tigrillo ('little tiger'), which is the common name for ocelots in South America although in fact they are spotted cats, about three times the size of a house-cat. He was as playful as a tabby cat, and as long as we kept clear of his needle-sharp teeth we had great fun frolicking around our room and the small hotel garden. The hotel manager looked mournful at the state of his flower beds but kindly procured for us a small female ocelot as a mate for Tigrillo.

We were delayed in Iquitos for many days, trying to get government permission to keep the animals we had collected. This involved endless consultations over a crackling radio telephone with our friend Felipe Benavides, the world-famous Peruvian naturalist, and visits to the local air force commander, who had charge of a small zoo at the base.

Charlie came everywhere with me. Since she was only about six weeks old and four inches long, and could easily fit into the palm of my hand, this was not difficult to manage. Charlie's favourite place was inside my sun-dress; it was a little disconcerting for strangers when she did bumps and grinds underneath and then hauled herself over the top and wriggled about from one of the straps.

At last we got word from Felipe that we would be allowed to bring Charlie and some other animals with us but would have to leave Tigrillo and his girl friend at the air force zoo. Reluctantly we took them back to the sympathetic air force colonel, who had helped to secure a 'passport' for Charlie. He promised to take care of them and to do everything possible to make the ocelots legitimate travellers too. He put them in a room with a half-grown capybara, a fat, hairy creature that looks like the missing link between guinea-pigs and hippopotami and is regarded with enthusiasm by fully grown jaguars and ocelots as a sort of walking butcher's shop.

Tigrillo, confronted with his parents' natural prey, was of course determined to show that he could perform like a full-grown ocelot. He stalked the capybara around the room with a glint in his yellowy eye. The capybara shuffled and snuffled, and appealed to us with doleful bleating sounds to relieve the situation. Then Tigrillo sprang: landing on the capybara's ample hind-quarters, he raked at it with his tiny claws. He was not big enough to do it much damage, but the colonel had the young capybara taken away to another pen. It can't be much fun sharing a room with someone who will take a meal-sized bite out of you when he grows big enough.

Alas, that was the last we saw of Tigrillo. The ocelots were never sent on to us as promised. We were told that they had died of a form of feline enteritis.

But Charlie prospered. Armed with the proper forms, we decided to take her to Lima with us on the plane. There was one hitch: it seemed unlikely that the airline was keen about carrying animals, even a baby tamarin. Charlie was already so dependent on me as her new mother that we felt sure she would die if she had to travel alone in the hold of the plane. So Charlie began her career as a stowaway. I popped her inside my sun-dress, where she was remarkably well-behaved throughout a long wait at the tiny local airport. She slept for most of the trip over the Andes.

When we got to Lima we went straight to the Bolivar Hotel; Charlie was moving up in the world. The Bolivar is a grand old hotel that might have been moved lock, stock and barrel from the Rue St-Honoré in Paris. Its doormen dress like admirals and its vast, colonnaded lobby is still a favourite with the local dowagers who arrive each afternoon for their *te ingles*.

I was not sure what our impeccable concierge would think about a tamarin at the Bolivar, so we devised elaborate schemes to keep Charlie well hidden. We bought a small basket in which we could carry her under a piece of towelling. Fearful that this ruse would not escape the curious eyes of the lift-boys, we took the staircase up and down to our rooms. I am sure that the hotel staff had spotted their new guest on the very first day, but they would no more have drawn attention to the fact than a well-bred Parisian hotel-keeper would have dreamed of commenting on the fact that a gentleman resident was in the habit of entertaining ladies in his room.

We made Charlie's bed in her basket, which we kept in the bathroom, well lined with a hotel towel. When she left the basket she spent much of the time riding about on my head, under my hat. She still loved foraging about in human hair and must have been disappointed not to find any lice in mine!

It was clear to us that we would not be able to ship Charlie back to England with the other animals we had bought. We seemed to have only one alternative: to smuggle her on to a plane. We didn't know whether there was any provision in airline regulations for baby monkeys. Charlie would not, of course, be an illegal immigrant: she had the papers we needed to get her out of Peru and into England. But we thought we were likely to get a dusty answer if we asked the airline whether we could take her with our hand-luggage. Could we really keep a highly strung monkey out of sight for fifteen hours or so?

While we got ready for our return trip, Charlie saw the sights and something of the social life of Lima. We found that John's grandfather, Admiral of the Fleet Jacky Fisher, was still revered by the Peruvian Navy. The commanders of the Peruvian fleet invited us to an official lunch; they wanted to toast Jacky Fisher and show off their new warships and submarines, of which they were fiercely proud. Charlie had barely been out of my sight since we bought her, but I had a moment's doubt about whether her social acceptability would extend to Peruvian admirals.

I asked Felipe, who was also coming to the lunch, whether we should leave Charlie at the zoo run by his sister, Carmen. He wouldn't hear of it. 'No, no,' he said. 'You'll see. They won't mind at all.'

So we set off with Charlie in her basket in the car. We left her there for a couple of hours while we were given a tour of the ships in the naval dockyard. By the time we were ready for lunch the sun was blazing hot and I began to worry that Charlie was being slowly grilled in the car. We had also travelled a long way from our starting-point. John bearded our host, an admiral, and asked whether we could go back to fetch Charlie. He did not explain who Charlie was, and it is doubtful whether the admiral had any inkling. 'But of course,' he insisted.

So John was taken back by the admiral's driver to rescue Charlie. Tamarins, like marmosets, are not celebrated for their even tempers. Charlie felt that she had been treated abominably and was determined to tell the world about it in a stream of monkey swearing that we suspected would have put a sailor to shame if we could only have translated her shrieks and trills. Her mood was not improved when John tried hanging her up in her little basket from a hat-stand outside the room where the lunch was being held. This did not accord with Charlie's view of her social place. Live admirals in dress uniform and moustachioed admirals and presidents long-dead who gazed down solemnly from the walls were treated to a deafening display of the range of her vocal chords. The commotion was so great that I realised there was no chance at all of normal conversation unless Charlie was invited to join us. I think the admiral was too flabbergasted by the suggestion to object. Charlie appeared with knitted brows but deigned to accept a comfortable seat on John's lap and was stuffed with rice and fruits.

She realised that her moment of revenge was at hand. When the admiral proposed a toast to John's grandfather, a slurping in the middle of the speech suggested that some-one had been unable to wait for a drink. The admiral glowered round the room to see who was the delinquent. His eyes came to rest, in a wide-eyed stare, on his wife. Charlie had got his head deep down inside her glass, slurping up what I suppose was brandy. There was a moment's pause before everybody burst out laughing.

I somehow doubt that the Peruvian Navy has entertained a small tamarin to an official lunch since then.

Feeding Charlie was still largely a matter of trial and error. Every monkey has individual tastes of its own, just like a human. A common mistake is to imagine that small monkeys must be vegetarians. On the contrary, tamarins and marmosets are great insect-eaters, thriving on the beetles, cockroaches and flying insects that they are able to catch in the middle storeys of their jungle skyscrapers. Charlie drank huge quantities of milk, which she could swallow by herself from a cup or saucer – unlike larger monkey species that take longer to mature and need to be bottle-fed for months if they have a human foster-mother. This early maturing suggests quick but also limited intelligence. Characteristically, the brainiest species (including man) require the longest mothering.

Charlie enjoyed cheese and many fruits but her great favourite was a rather grisly delicacy: mosquitoes gorged with our blood. She would pounce on slow-moving mosquitoes that had just had their dinner at our expense but would spit out with disgust others that we caught for her before they bit us.

It was not until we got Charlie-girl back to England that we found that she regarded live spiders as the supreme gourmet experience. Every time a big spider crawled out of the plughole in one of our baths, as they so often seem to do in an old house, cries of horror from the children would be followed by the shout, 'Quick, get Charlie!' Charlie would pounce upon the unfortunate spider, crunch up the body and then fastidiously spit out the legs, for all the world like a man eating a bony fish. Spiders are not one of my favourite creatures, but they supplied a diet that saved John and me from having to contribute to Charlie's meal with our own blood!

We found a more civilised way of supplying Charlie with her red meat in Lima, although she missed the joy of the chase. In restaurants, we would order a steak and ask for a corner of it to be served raw. With a shrug and a mutter in the kitchen about those inexplicable foreigners, the maître d'hôtel would usually oblige.

The day of our flight back to England finally arrived. We started out for the airport with Charlie comfortably ensconced in her little basket. Before we got there I put her on my head and crammed my sun-hat down over her.

This proved to be a simple way to smuggle a monkey through airport controls. Today, of course, airport security guards are increasingly inclined to feel you all over for concealed weapons, but I have never yet had my hat or my hair searched. We got Charlie safely on the plane, although our nerves were jangling. Sitting there waiting for take-off, with my seat belt fastened and a straw hat on my head, I felt a complete twit.

'I must look like the complete tourist,' I whispered to John.

'Don't think you're alone,' he said, as he stuffed a battered Panama on to his own head.

By the time we reached Bogotá, my watch (which I kept on Peruvian time to keep track of Charlie's accustomed meal-times) showed she was ready for her supper. As the seat-belt signs flashed on, I transferred her to the basket and sneaked her cheese and bananas. She squeaked with delight and embarked on a long conversation about her reactions to air travel. I do mean 'conversation'; tamarins and marmosets have an astonishingly wide vocabulary that can convey all sorts of precise information to those who understand it. I was nervous that the other passengers would hear but John rustled the newspaper we were holding over her basket and coughed furiously. When she had eaten enough, Charlie curled up again in her basket, cuddling the little toy llama we had bought for her in Lima.

But after Bogotá we found that our troubles had just begun. As the plane neared Caracas, the pilot's voice crackled apologetically over the intercom. 'I am sorry, ladies and gentlemen, but we have received information that there may be a bomb on the plane. This is probably a hoax, but I would ask you all to remain seated until we land at Caracas. I am afraid that we will then have to require all of you to disembark and identify your luggage while the plane is searched. This will mean a delay in our onward journey.'

My heart jumped, not because of the bomb scare but because the search posed the imminent threat that Charlie would be discovered. When the plane landed and the other passengers started to disembark, I said to John, 'You go on,

I'm going to stay on board.' The stewardess was obviously distracted so I said to her that I was feeling ill. Could I possibly stay on board while my husband got off the plane and identified our luggage? In her state of confusion, she said 'Certainly,' and left me sitting there.

But as security guards filed through the plane, searching for a bomb, they suddenly spotted me, the only passenger left on board. They were horrified. An officer rushed up and told me that I must get off immediately since the plane could blow up at any moment. Reluctantly I disembarked with Charlie's basket in one hand under my coat, which I hoped would make it invisible, and my handbag and face-case in the other.

I found that the passengers had been lined up in two long queues, the women in one, the men in the other. Everyone was being searched very thoroughly. I felt still more nervous. John came up to me, looking distinctly grey. Both of us were convinced that Charlie was now certain to be discovered. There was no opportunity to switch her back to my head without being spotted. I gave John my face-case to carry. When he reached the head of his queue, all that he had with him was a collection of make-up, lipstick and powder. The security guards looked at him quizzically, obviously convinced that he was *that* sort of Englishman.

I lingered behind, hoping that I might be forgotten in the rush. No such luck. I found that I was to be searched by a huge black man with hands like steam shovels. He went through everything. When he had searched my coat and my handbag, he pointed to the basket and ordered me to open it up. I thought my knees were going to collapse as his great fist descended into it. His fingers probed and I could imagine that Charlie, roused from her sleep, must be wriggling like mad.

I was overwhelmed by the thought that Charlie would now be detected, that she would be taken away from me and they would either kill her or put her in some place where

27

she would die anyway. I couldn't bear the thought that, after all we had been through, I was about to lose her.

The guard's expression suddenly suggested that he had just put his hand into some revolting mess and was uncertain what to do with it. Before he could ask me a question, I burst out spontaneously, 'Oh, please don't hurt it. It's my baby.'

The black security guard stared at me with saucer-eyes and turned a perceptibly greenish hue. He pulled his hand out as if he had been scalded and hissed, 'Take it away, for God's sake, take it away.' I am sure he thought that I had given birth to some unnatural thing on the plane.

The guard waved me on disgustedly. John seized my arm and we staggered back on board the plane and settled into a couple of stiff drinks.

We never did find out whether there had really been a bomb on the plane. Maybe the airline never did either, since in the final rush a big pile of luggage, including ours, was left unidentified and unsearched. The hostesses asked us not to mention the bomb scare so as not to upset the new passengers embarking at Caracas.

Charlie must have been even more exhausted than we were, since she slept all the way to Heathrow. In London she became legitimate again. My daughter, Trina, and my small granddaughter, Pandora, were waiting for us at the airport. Pandora whooped with joy when I opened my coat and a small monkey head popped out from underneath. For months afterwards, she would pull open my coat to see whether the same thing would happen. We then had to part with Charlie for six months while she went into quarantine. We would visit her from time to time and feel similar pangs to a parent visiting a child at boarding school.

Then we were finally able to bring Charlie home to Kilverstone. Charlie treated the house like the jungle. The tops of bookcases and doors, the edges of tables and chairs, the banisters and curtain-rails, all became forest boughs.

Charlie would lie on her tummy, like a squirrel, along the top of a door, limbs akimbo on either side. She would hang from the arm of a chair, waiting in ambush for a dog to pass by.

As she became more and more adventurous, she started to insist on keeping her own hours and not settling down at night until she was ready. One evening after dinner, one of our guests implored us to produce Charlie, who had been persuaded to bed down in her basket inside a cage that we kept in the sitting-room. No sooner had Charlie been woken up and removed from the cage than she started tearing round the room. She eventually perched on top of a bookcase, adamant that she would not go back to bed before we did.

Our guest was rather embarrassed but I reassured her that it was a familiar occurrence and went downstairs to watch the men play snooker in the billiards room. When I came up again, I found our guest relaxing in front of the fire with her hand resting on Charlie's basket.

'I managed to get her back,' she said. 'I must admit I used a small incentive.'

I peeped inside the basket and found Charlie fast asleep, flanked by no less than four liqueur glasses containing the remains of crème de menthe, cherry brandy, cointreau and brandy. She had clearly collapsed dead drunk. Was Charlie becoming a case for Alcoholics Anonymous? I took advantage of her condition to whisk away her booze and put the basket back inside the cage.

The next morning, we found that Charlie was suffering from a condition that is not unknown to humans. She had an almighty hangover. There was an anguished squeak from the basket as I drew the curtains and let the sunlight in. As Charlie's little face popped out from under her blanket, she clamped her tiny hands to her head. She glowered at me all morning as if she considered mankind to be the root of all evil.

Charlie became more and more absorbed into the family. She quickly learned to recognise our footsteps as we walked along the passages and would call out to each of us in a different way. We would hump her cage around with us from the library to the kitchen to the orangery, and outside in fine weather. Charlie's special playmate was my chihuahua called Tia, and it was not long before she was riding about on Tia's back like a miniature horseman. They became the best of friends, wrestling with each other and gambolling all over the house.

But after a year or so at Kilverstone, Charlie's character abruptly changed. She took a strong aversion to men. I don't know whether this may have been because she was resenting the absence of a male tamarin but one day, without provocation, Charlie shot across the library towards Charles, my youngest son, and sank her little teeth into his foot and his hand. We sent her to bed in disgrace. But the following evening the same thing happened again. Charles, who had been staying for the weekend, decided to beat a tactical retreat to London.

John was greatly amused by the episode, which gave rise to much banter about how Charles, who had been thinking of training to be a zoo curator, had fallen out with his animal relations. John insisted that it would be perfectly safe to let Charlie out again the next day. This was when Charlie made her fatal mistake.

No sooner had her cage been opened than she streaked up the stairs, bowled into our bedroom, darted up John's trouser leg, and bit him high up on his inside thigh — fortunately, not quite so high up as might have been. This was the end of the road for Charlie. At Kilverstone a jungle baby can get away with a great deal. My children often complain, in fact, that baby monkeys are treated far more lightly than they were at a similiar stage. But no jungle baby can get away with biting John inside the house.

Perhaps Charlie sensed that she had had her last fling.

She certainly seemed to have decided to make the most of it. After biting John, she whooshed out of the door and down the driveway, where she encountered an unsuspecting, near-sighted mechanic who was fixing our car. Without a second's hesitation, she gave him a couple of determined nips on the leg, He complained afterwards that he had been assaulted by a stoat.

John's mind was made up: Charlie must be banished. We put her in a cage at the foot of the old water tower, in the macaw garden. She has neighbours who speak her own language: two tamarins called Minnie and Tammy. Better still, Minnie has given birth to twins at Kilverstone (marmosets and tamarins usually have litters of two), one of whom will provide a mate for Charlie. After the twins were born, Tammy proved himself to be the model of the domesticated male. Every women's libber would be delighted by him. He spent most of his time caring for the babies, carrying them about on his shoulders and only handing them over to their mother when they needed milk.

Charlie never quite forgave us for expelling her from the house. She sulked for a long time, taking food from my hand with her head turned – just to show that she was not going to be bribed that easily – and delivering long sermons to the public on the great wrong that had been done to her.

3

Feeding a Family on Steak Tartare

Imagine feeding a family of hundreds on fruit salad and steak tartare every day! Imagine that most of them are also neurotic about the cold, so that you have to pay for central heating – underfloor or overhead, depending on their tastes – even on what any normal Englishman would consider a decent spring day. You can then begin to grasp the sort of costs that are involved in maintaining the extended family of a wildlife park in the style which they demand. We found that it cost us about £1 a day to feed just one monkey. Needless to say, the person who took the keenest interest in these figures (after John, who had to burn the midnight oil night after night in his wilderness of a study) was the bank manager. And one thing can be said about the price of any necessity in a Britain riddled with inflation: what goes up, goes up again.

Back from the fun and games of the safari on which we found Charlie monkey, we had to face up to the grim realities of trying to make ends meet. We did not set out to make Kilverstone into a Latin American zoo in any expectation of making a fortune. At the same time, we did not have pots of money to sink into subsidising the park – and if we had had, the taxman would no doubt have spirited them away. No, the aim had to be to get the park on a footing where it could pay for itself. 'Money in the bank,' as John put it, 'is not just a saying. It's an expression of contentment and an index of success and above all a sound foundation on which to lay plans for the future.' Money in the bank was what, sooner or later, the park would have to produce if we were going to be able to keep it open.

To some people, the idea of trying to make a wildlife park financially viable – except on the most vulgarised, commercial basis, and very close to one of the great cities – sounds rather quixotic. But we were not indulging in a wild gamble. We were confident that we could make a go of Kilverstone commercially without having to become commercialised. We abhorred the idea of turning the place into a sort of amusement arcade or of restricting our collection of animals to a few exotic specimens that would titillate the casual visitor without offering any real insight into the wealth of species that inhabit the jungles and plains and waterways of Latin America. We were ready to put our shoulders to the wheel. We thought we had an ideal environment at Kilverstone and the location – just off a main road and within a comfortable drive from the rapidly expanding towns of Bury St Edmunds, King's Lynn, Norwich, Newmarket and Cambridge – seemed promising, even if the local council was awkward about letting us put up signs beside the road.

So John sat down with his accountants and made his calculations. The magic figure turned out to be 100,000. That was the number of visitors we would need in a year in order to break even. The idea of attracting enough people to fill Wembley Stadium was daunting, but by now we were thoroughly committed to the challenge and pressed on with our plans. Our aim was to achieve the 100,000 target within three years.

One of our first tasks was to find a curator. We had met a big, bearded, red-cheeked Scotsman called Brian Dickson when he was working for the wildlife park in the west country which had first inspired us. Not the least of Brian's talents is that he sees auras around people's heads. As a child he considered this quite normal: 'I never asked why the saints in religious paintings had haloes around their heads,' he told me, 'because I see haloes around people's heads all the time.' It seems that the colour of the aura changes depending on both your state of health and how good or wicked you have been. The lowest you can get, according to Brian, is a sort of dirty orange. I made him promise never to tell me if he saw me sporting such a disreputable aura.

This cheerful eccentric became the park's curator and arrived at Kilverstone in the winter of 1972. His great passion was wild birds and he had come up to Norfolk six weeks ahead of his wife, Jean, to help us put up our aviaries. We put him in a spare bedroom named after one of Admiral Fisher's ships, the *Furious*. Unluckily for Brian, we were keeping Sniffles, a coatimundi, and two macaws in the room below. The macaws will chew up almost anything with their great hooked beaks, and they soon got to work on the ceiling and chomped some large holes through the plaster and the packing under Brian's floor. Macaws have a distinctive smell of their own, sweet and sickly like rotting mangoes. This earned Brian an unfortunate reputation for a while. Valerie, who helps us about the house, made me go up and smell Brian's room one day. 'Phew,' she said, 'I think he's been with the birds too long.'

Although Brian started out as a bird man, he soon developed an affection for the monkeys and in particular the sloths, who were among the first arrivals at Kilverstone. Indeed, Brian developed into a staunch defender of the sloth in the face of the familiar allegations that it is one of nature's bone-idle creatures.

'They may be slothful, as the name suggests, in the course of their daily lives,' Brian will argue, 'but you should see them move if they get really angry. I once had to go into the cage belonging to Slow Jo and Bottoms Up' – our pair of three-toed sloths – 'to repair their heating system. I gingerly moved the female from her perch in order to get at the radiator. She's an absolute poppit and made no fuss, but Slow Jo was furious to see me taking liberties with his wife. To my horror, he slid halfway down his tree-trunk in seconds, obviously bent on taking a swipe at me. I started backing off, but only in the nick of time. Before I knew it, he was swinging from the lower part of his tree-trunk and there was a great swishing sound as his two big forepaws closed over each other like scissors in front of my nose. Never underrate a sloth when its temper is up.'

Apart from being nibble-prone – few of our birds or animals, including the peaceable falabella miniature horses, seemed to be able to resist taking a peck or a bite out of the seat of Brian's trousers whenever the chance came their way – and prone to seeing auras around people's heads, Brian had as many brushes with the public as any of us. It fell to him to act the policeman's part when serious crimes such as wilful scattering of litter were taking place. It is just as well that he is a good-natured, patient Scot, because he was often enough confronted with situations that would have made me blow my top.

Not long after we opened, Brian was collecting litter after one of his rounds and passed close to a family out for an afternoon's relaxation who stood idly by, watching him snatch up the cellophane bags and empty cans. After several minutes of watching Brian darting back and forth to the nearest rubbish-bin, the father of the family pulled a packet of cigarettes from his pocket, tore off the cellophane and openly deposited it on the ground, then ripped out the silver paper, shredded it and dropped that too. Brian's normally russet complexion turned to a menacing beetroot. But all he said was, 'Look here, sir, there is a litter basket just there.'

The visitor had the gall to reply, 'It's all right, brother. Just think, if it wasn't for people like myself who chuck the litter on the ground, your lot would be unemployed.'

Brian was overcome by a bout of temporary laryngitis. It was just as well, I suppose, that he found himself speechless.

The other new arrivals at Kilverstone before the opening, besides Brian and the animals, were the half-dozen keepers we recruited from far and wide. Some were local lads without previous experience of wild animals. But they were keen to learn, fond of their charges and, above all, most of them had the indispensable qualification for working at Kilverstone: a sense of humour. In the early days of the park, the favourite butt for most of the keepers was a very earnest boy from Thetford called Paul, who looked after the outside paddocks. Paul was a keen rugby player and would always rush about as if he was intending to practise a tackle, wearing a little woollen cap with a pom-pom, exactly like a tea-cosy. He also sported a beard but seemed rather uncertain about it, since he would shave it off every few months and then let it sprout back again.

I think that the meanest trick the keepers played on Paul was to present him with a bucket of sprats one afternoon, just before the penguins' feeding hour. Peter, the head keeper and Brian Dickson's number two, a strapping west country boy who is a bird fanatic and takes special pride in his aviaries, ceremoniously passed the bucket to Paul.

'Right, you'd better get on with gutting these,' he said.

Now, a sprat is only about two inches long, and to dissect one would be a task worthy of a micro-biologist. But half an hour later, when Peter walked back into the keepers' kitchen, he discovered that Paul was still studiously trying to gut the bucketful of sprats.

Another of the keepers, a little Welshman called Roy, took charge of the hardbill birds. Together with Geoffrey, a very cheerful, dedicated keeper who made himself a genuine expert on wild cats, and the other young men who worked at Kilverstone, Roy would spend many of his evenings at the club on the estate that had been established by the staff and local farmers in the old farmhouse made available by John. My younger son, Charles, would often meet up with them there over a game of darts, a pint of the local bitter or one of the powerful concoctions – like rum-and-blackcurrant – that Norfolk country folk seem to favour.

By Charles's account, Roy would keep fairly much to himself, sitting quietly in a corner, working his way patiently through a beer. But one evening Charles and the other keepers put him through his paces. The following morning, John ran into Roy in the park, looking distinctly green about the gills and wandering around with a bucket in his hand. An hour later, he was still carrying the same bucket. As lunchtime approached, his hand was still attached to the bucket as if someone had stuck them together with a superglue.

'Hey, Roy,' one of the keepers called, 'what have you got that bucket for?'

'Just in case I take sick,' came the lilting reply. I suppose it was a rational answer.

My John, Brian and John the butler – a former seaman with an inexhaustible supply of sailor's jokes – all turned into carpenters and bricklayers as we worked to get the cages set up. We had picked up a few rules of thumb by studying what had gone right and wrong at other zoos. We knew, for example, that a quick way to turn a healthy animal into a neurotic is to shut it up in a cage with few things to amuse it and nowhere for it to hide away from the public when it is feeling anti-social.

So we built every animal cage with two bedrooms, one for the male and one for the female, so that they could get into a warm, private place whenever they wanted and away from each other, too: human beings aren't the only people who have marital ups and downs. We built octagonal cages for the big cats – the jaguars, pumas and bobcats. We built the parrot cage in the shape of a Maltese cross. Some of the early cages we built had a homely look, with overhanging roofs rather like the 'halts' that you can still find beside railway lines in quiet parts of the countryside. One day when Brian came back from lunch, he found that the keepers had painted the words 'Dickson's Halt' on the roof of the cage on which he had been working.

We had to think a lot about heating. At home in the tropics, our birds and animals had never experienced anything like a Norfolk winter. We arranged everything so that they could stay in or out of the cold as they pleased, like humans. We were surprised by how hardy some of them turned out to be, and you will see flamingos paddling about in the depths of winter; the only thing to be wary of is to prevent them from getting trapped if the water ices over.

We were innocent at first about heat conservation but we did know that you have to be careful about where you put the heating units. Underfloor heating is marvellous for quick-moving, high climbing animals like monkeys but it can be literally lethal for slow-moving creatures. A giant tortoise died in an English zoo as a result of over-heating from a unit below the floor; the autopsy described it as cooked meat. So when we built a house for the capybaras, we put the heating unit in the roof. It's not the cheapest way to heat a room but we didn't fancy serving up baby capybara for lunch. While all the hammering and sawing was going on, I was tending to Charlie, getting to know some of our other new arrivals and helping them to settle down in their new houses. This is probably the most important chore in any zoo.

Soon after we came home with Charlie, we took delivery of a pair of Brazilian tapirs that we called Marcus and Malu after two Brazilian friends of ours in the diplomatic service. We were very glad to get them, since most of the surviving types of tapir are listed in the *Red Book* of wildlife in danger as being on the verge of extinction. The tapir is an odd survivor from prehistoric times, when it ranged freely over the great plains of Central Asia and North America. Today, three of the four surviving species are to be found in Central and South America. Few explorers of the rain-forest have seen a family of tapirs or even a pair. All that most travellers have been able to glimpse is a solitary tapir picking its lonely way through the jungle.

Tapirs have the reputation of being shy, retiring creatures, frightened of man. They have good reason to be, since man has so often come upon them in the wild with a spear or a blowdart or a gun. They have been widely hunted for their tough hides, ideal for making whips or bridles. The tapir flourished for millions of years, despite its almost complete defencelessness against familiar predators like the jaguar, until man arrived and began to destroy its native habitat.

It would be sad to see it disappear. If you can imagine a cross between a rhinoceros, a donkey and a wild boar, you will have some idea of what it looks like. Its most remarkable feature is its nose, which hangs over its lower jaw in a short trunk. It stretches it out and curls it back like a child's paper whistle. This Pinocchio nose enables it to sniff its way through the dark forest. The tapir lives by smell rather than sight, and while its nose has swollen up and expanded, its eyes are reduced to little piggy ones set back in deep sockets. The tapir's nose, slightly swollen at the tip, has other uses. Like a chubby sensitive finger, it can stretch up and down to pull off leaves and shoots that are out of reach of its teeth.

The tapir also has a mane of short, stiff hair, reaching from the top of its head to its shoulders. The experts speculate that this was developed, through evolution, as a partial defence against the jaguar, which has an unpleasant habit of leaping on to the tapir's back from an overhanging bough. According to this argument, when the jaguar tries to sink its powerful teeth into the tapir's neck muscles, all it comes away with is a mouthful of hair – giving the tapir time to canter off into the safety of thicker forest or a nearby stream. I have never seen this happen, but if that is all the tapir has to rely on, I would not give much for its chances of making a safe getaway.

The tapir looks more like a pig than a horse (although the horse is its cousin) with its short, stocky neck, its high rump and its thickset, fleshy body. It can weigh as much as 750 lb. and leaves punched footprints in the ground like an elephant – with the difference that the tapir has only three toes on its forefeet and four splayed toes on its hind feet. But it can move with astonishing speed and grace through even the densest vegetation. It is also a marvellous swimmer. A tapir will spend hours on end lazing about in the water. It loves the mud even more and can plough its way through ooze that no other sensible beast would think of treading on. Brazilian tapirs have been known to lie about, completely covered with mud, like a woman with a face-pack. The reason is probably not vanity but the desire to keep the insects at bay.

We were especially pleased with our girl tapir, Malu, who was a stunning honey-blonde, a colour that is very rare amongst tapirs. She also had a marvellous disposition, squatting down on the ground and squeaking with delight when I tickled her tummy. We learned from Malu that tapirs soon lose their fear of humans if they are treated with love and affection.

But sadly she was not in good health. The vet found that Malu had an abscess on her throat which had begun to poison her whole system. It was the same infection that is known in horses as strangles. He decided to operate at once but either the anaesthetic was too strong or the shock was too great for her, because she died while she was still unconscious.

It was our first death at Kilverstone, and we were bitterly unhappy. We made it one of our first tasks to find a new bride for Marcus. Fortunately, it was not long before we were able to take delivery of another female tapir. She arrived as a child-bride, looking exactly like a mint humbug, covered with white spots and symmetrical stripes. Tapirs lose this perfect camouflage for the patchy half-light of the rainforest after the age of about six months.

We built Marcus and his new mate a very comfortable semi-detached bungalow down in the water meadows. It stood up on a platform so that when the rains came, flooding the meadows and raising the level of the river until it lapped over the boathouse, far back from the shore, the tapirs could sit like Venetian doges, surveying the watery world where they are most at home, or slither down for a swim. Every night when the river was at its height, Marcus would go off on a long moonlight paddle.

In the midst of our troubles with Malu the tapir, our first flamingos arrived. The dealer drove up in a spanking new Jensen – buying and selling animals is clearly more lucrative than keeping them! There was not a flamingo in sight and I thought at first that something had gone wrong. Then the dealer opened his boot to reveal what looked, from a distance, like a family of pink cobras swaying their heads to and fro over the top of their wicker baskets.

'The only way to travel with these birds,' he explained, 'is to fold them up carefully and pop their legs into nylon stockings. If you don't stop them from thrashing about, they can snap their legs like matchsticks.'

I was so astonished by the sight of flamingos in stockings that I dashed inside to get John and the children to come and look. Charles was the first to come running downstairs, wearing his favourite vivid-red-and-yellow Texaco jacket that makes him look like a petrol pump attendant who is frightened of getting run over in the dark.

But by the time Charles got out into the drive, one of the flamingos had already managed to untangle itself from its hosiery and had set off down the drive, apparently bent on seeing the sights of Thetford. It moved with the stiff, determined gait of a long-distance walker, but at a speed that would put an average runner through his paces.

Charles is no Olympic runner but he manfully gave chase down the winding driveway and out on to the road, where he was soon overtaken by a busload of American tourists. They were delighted to be served an example of typical British eccentricity on a country road; perhaps they thought that flamingo-chasing was on their programme. The bus slowed down to keep pace with Charles, windows were rolled down and blue-rinsed ladies and men in check coats with lots of cameras whistled and applauded as Charles puffed along behind the bird, his face by now as pink as the flamingo's plumage.

'My money's on the bird,' someone shouted.

'Say, do you do this all the time, or only on weekends?'

With a final spurt, Charles managed to get close enough to the bird to grab it. Winded but triumphant, he had the grace to take a small bow, the flamingo clasped in both arms, while the Americans whistled and clapped.

'I'm coming back for the matinée,' someone called.

'Come back on 1 April,' said Charles.

It was our first escape, and – unwittingly – our first publicity stunt.

But by the end of our first year it was depressingly obvious that we would have to do more than amuse a passing busload of American tourists if the park was going to survive.

It fell to John to make the periodic visits to the bank manager. He was not one of those forbidding figures who are prone to emitting jaguar-like sounds at the mention of a possible extension of an overdraft. He liked animals and was himself an enthusiast for the park. All the same, his trade required cold statistics, precise projections.

On his visit to the bank at the end of our first year, John had the unpleasant task of reporting that we had failed to achieve our starting target of 60,000 visitors in our first season. We had been over-optimistic. We had also learned the hard way that running a wildlife park is a business that is dependent, like most of the leisure trade, on the vagaries of British weather, especially over Bank Holiday weekends, when millions of families wondering how to amuse restless children on the third day off work hop into their cars and take to the roads. The pattern of seasonal trade that was quickly established at Kilverstone was a large crowd over Easter, followed by a fairly dull month in the run-up to the Spring Bank Holiday and then a moderate increase in visitors, working up to the real holiday season in late July, August and early September. Wet Bank Holidays or a cold, early Easter could spell disaster to our budget.

In our first year, when we still had everything to learn, we had started out well enough at Easter and over the Spring Bank Holiday, but the hoped-for crowds did not materialise in the summer vacations and we were left to survive the long winter recess, during which potential visitors curl up at home and watch the telly – a winter with no receipts coming in but with more bills to be met, not just for the upkeep of what we had started but for the expansion we wanted to carry out and which we knew would help to draw in more visitors.

John talked hopefully to the bank manager about bigger crowds in the year ahead, arguing that because of rising wages more people in Britain would be spending more money than ever before on leisure activities such as wild-life parks. Whether or not our bank manager accepted these theories, he was very tolerant. He tactfully avoided reminding John of one or two little snags that had cropped up: for example, the fact that the price of heating had trebled. The bank would go on backing us.

By contrast, John's accountant put on his most dour manner. 'There's going to be another winter after this one, you know,' he bleakly reminded John. 'How, if I may ask, do you propose to pay your way through that one?'

John could only mutter something about having to think it over.

The accountant scratched his chin and said solemnly, 'You'd better sell some land.'

We were driving to London that day and John set off in a glum mood. We were going to collect our first ora pendola, that beautiful, olive-green bird of the jungle with the golden tail and the unforgettable call. The ora pendola (who was soon to acquire the nickname of Dolly Bird from the keepers, which didn't quite fit since it was a he) was very friendly from first acquaintance, happiest of all when sitting on my head or shoulders. We put him in a cardboard box for the drive up to Kilverstone so that I could sit close to him and tickle his feathers if he took fright from the unfamiliar motion of the car. But I made the mistake of not keeping the opening in the box where I put my hand through tightly closed. Before I knew what was happening, Dolly Bird had slid out of the box and joined us in the front seat for a more intimate conversation.

If he had just wanted to perch on my shoulder, that might have been all right. But ora pendolas crave to be the centre of attention. Dolly Bird ensured that no one would ignore his presence by flattening himself across the inside of the windscreen, wings outstretched. All John could see, as we belted up the A1 motorway towards the Cambridge turn-off, was the inside of Dolly Bird's armpit. Furthermore, since we were in the middle lane with cars on our left, we could not simply swing off the road.

'Don't frighten it,' said John. 'Don't do anything sudden.'

'*I'm* the one who's frightened,' I moaned.

At this point Sam, our golden labrador retriever, decided to take charge of the situation. His training as a retriever had not gone very far. In fact, training seemed to have little effect on most of our Kilverstone retrievers, who were well-meaning but seldom seemed to get the bird – or if they did, might take a bite or two out of it. After picking up one or two pheasants that the dogs had missed, I got the reputation of being 'John's number one gun-dog'. Whatever his educational defects, however, Sam knew by instinct that that thing fluttering across the windscreen must be a quarry.

Rising from his slumbers on the back seat, Sam did a good imitation of a pointer, obviously convinced that we had organised the appearance of the curious thing in the front in order to test his reflexes. Before I had time to order 'Down, Sam!' he had leaped forward over the back of John's seat, colliding with John's left shoulder, and was making dog-paddling movements in mid-air above the steering wheel, his teeth bared to sink into Dolly Bird.

His sense of timing was impressive. As John involuntarily swerved towards the left-hand lane, I saw a huge container lorry drawing up beside us. 'Watch out, darling,' I screamed. Swinging the wheel back to the right while trying to shoulder Sam out of the way, John was overtaken by a little red MG sports car with one of those maddening 'sucks-to-you' horns. Luckily for us, John has a steady hand at the wheel. He ploughed on while I tried to separate Sam and Dolly Bird. I finally got Sam back on to the back seat, and folded Dolly Bird up like a collapsible chair, back inside his box.

'Whew!' said John. 'That was a close one. If we can get through that, I think we can beat the accountants yet.'

There was a throaty rumble from Sam, intent on sniffing at Dolly Bird's box. I squeezed John's hand.

4

Panama and
Spider Monkeys

Each year since the opening of the park, John and I have
made at least one foray back to South America in search
of new animals. We acquired some extraordinary friends,
both animal and human. After our first year, when we
had persuaded the bank manager and ourselves that we
were really going to make a go of Kilverstone, we flew out
to Panama, where we made friends with the Gale family.

Nate Gale was a dedicated American vet, married to a
tall, willowy blonde called Ellie. We found them living in a
house built high up on stilts with cages underneath to hold
part of their animal collection. Ellie took us to the kitchen,
opened the window and in walked a margay, a small, spotted
wild cat. It had the run of the house, exactly like a cat, but
no one would have dared to use the word 'pet' of any wild
animal in that household.

One of Nate's accomplishments had been to rear a maned
wolf in San Francisco Zoo, one of the first maned wolves
that had ever been reared successfully in captivity. The
maned wolf is one of the most striking predators of the New
World. It stands about thirty inches high at the shoulder
on very long, delicate legs. With its big ears, pointed,

quivering muzzle and razor edge reflexes, the maned wolf seems to live on its nerves. Its basic diet – surprising to people who think that wolves are essentially carnivores – is fruit and vegetables, although it will prey upon birds, reptiles, insects, and a few smaller animals. Hearing his story and poring over photographs, we resolved that we must bring a pair of maned wolves to Kilverstone. If we could find them, they would be the only maned wolves kept in Britain.

The Gales spent their weekends driving into the outskirts of the Darien jungles between Panama and the south and would hack their way onward on foot or take a small boat with an outboard motor along the rivers. Some of the densest jungle of Central America is to be found here, a natural sanctuary for animals that have fled the bulldozers elsewhere. We went trekking into the jungle and came back with some crab-eating raccoons which we prevailed upon the Gales to keep for us until we returned to England.

After our talks with the Gales, we were particularly keen to get to Barro Colorado, an island in the Panama Canal that is the home of one of the world's finest natural wildlife reserves.

The island is actually the top of a mountain which was submerged when the Chagres river was dammed during the construction of the Panama Canal. Although it covers an area of only about 4,000 acres, it is thickly forested and contains more than 250 kinds of birds and some 60 species of mammals, not to mention thousands of insects – unfortunately including the stinging and burrowing kinds. Since the early 1920s, Barro Colorado island has been the stamping-ground of the Smithsonian Institution, the remarkable research organisation whose headquarters in Washington look like a cross between a Victorian brewery and a Scottish feudal keep. The Smithsonian scientists use the island as a zoological research station.

We climbed out of bed before dawn in Panama City and

took the train down to the halt beside Lake Gaitan, where we were picked up by a launch to take us to the island. On the other side of the lake we had to face a sinew-stretching climb up more than 200 steps to where our hosts, Dr Mike Robinson and his wife, were awaiting us. Mike Robinson is a genial Englishman who spent much of his life in Canada and whose speciality is entomology. His professional obsession is with spiders – not one that appeals to me!

'I do hope you keep your creepy-crawlies in a safe place,' I said, when I heard what he was working on.

He laughed it off. 'I think you'll find plenty of other things to amuse you,' he said.

Filled up with coffee and sprayed all over with insect repellent in an effort to protect ourselves against the omni-present ticks, we set off with the Robinsons down a jungle path. It was the veteran who turned out to be the first victim of our little expedition. While we were trying to sight a toucan that we could hear calling through the foliage, Mike Robinson was stung by an inch-long black ant, one of the sort that can paralyse a man with its bite. Fortunately, the effect of this one sting proved to be nothing more than a sudden yelp of pain, followed by a persistent ache. We plunged on and soon came upon the sounds and smells of a herd of collared peccaries that we could hear scampering away through the forest.

Seeing a sudden movement in the branches of a big wild fig tree, Mike gestured to us to stop. He led us off the trail for a few paces into the forest and motioned to us to look through the trees. We were rewarded with a spectacle of a troupe of black howler monkeys, eight or ten of them, lazing about in the branches of the wild fig tree 100 feet above the ground like people lounging in hammocks, munching their favourite fruit. When they became aware of our presence they responded with the ear-splitting, booming roar that has been likened to the angry call of all the jaguars in the forest. The howler monkeys use their extraordinary roar to mark out their territorial rights and to frighten away enemies – and it must work in the case of those who have never heard it before since it seems impossibly loud for an animal of their size. Particularly at sunrise and sunset, different troupes can be heard calling and answering.

On our return hike we stumbled across some agoutis – a sort of large, tail-less, long-legged rat – and a tovi parakeet, which shot out of its nest in a hole in a dead tree. We had a languid, pleasurable lunch, during which the Robinsons regaled us with tales of the island, and decided to retire for a quick siesta since we had been asked to stay the night. We were aroused within an hour or so with cries of 'The spiders are here'.

I jerked awake and clutched hold of John. 'What's happening?' I demanded. 'Are Mike's pet tarantulas on the loose?' I squeaked with fright when I saw that there was indeed a very large and hairy spider squatting on the window-sill.

Happily, however, we had not been summoned to look at real spiders: from the verandah we could see that a troupe of monkeys had arrived. There were half a dozen of these rare Panamanian spider monkeys with black backs and nutty brown tummies and, as it turned out, they were males. They had become tame enough to visit the kitchen from time to time to raid the larder. As with most animal species, spider monkeys will not tolerate any nonsense about women's lib. The males arrived first to enjoy the choicest pickings. Half an hour or so later, when they had had plenty of time to eat their fill, their women folk turned up with the babies to pick over anything that was left. After they had all finished their snack, they crossed through the camp and swung up into the big trees on the western slope of the valley in which our little settlement was located. They seemed to be heading for a massive old tree, standing at least 150 feet high.

As I watched them climbing up into it, I suddenly

glimpsed a strange, metallic-looking object the shape of a pyramid jutting up from the topmost branches of the tree. I shifted a few yards to get a view of it from a different angle and found to my astonishment that what I was looking at was a big iguana, perhaps seven or eight feet long, mottled with light and dark green splodges and with the strange triangular spinal scales clearly visible. I had always thought iguanas lived on the ground but it seems that they will climb even very tall trees to get at the tender leaves on the topmost branches. One day we hope to have a reptile house at Kilverstone and iguanas will be among its first inhabitants.

More animals turned up to join our supper. Some coatis came right into the kitchen looking for scraps. Sitting out on the verandah of the mess-hall as the sun set over the Pacific, we watched the birds catapult across the horizon. We mulled over the strange inhabitants, both human and animal, of the country. They included legendary figures such as Tio Hermann, the mysterious German who led a hermit-like existence in the wilds of the Darien forest along Panama's southern border and was reputed to be a former high-ranking Nazi who had fled his past as far away from civilisation as he could get. Every so often, when he ran short of supplies, he would round up a few of the cattle that he raised in the depths of the wilderness, tie a rope around their horns and lead them three days' march to the nearest village to exchange them for provisions.

Uplifted by the wine, the good company and the vibrant animal noises coming from the forest, we sank into bed early: I fell into a perfect, dreamless sleep, to be aroused by John at a quarter to five.

'Shhhh!' he hissed with his finger to his lips. He tiptoed out on to the verandah, motioning to me to follow. Moaning and groaning, I stumbled out after him. I found that a family of the rare Central American Baird's tapirs were snuffling along between the stilts on which our guest-house stood, picking over the grass and leaves with their long, rubbery snouts. It seemed that they were the first guests to arrive for breakfast since they wended their way up the hill to the cookhouse, where they milled patiently about behind the back door until the cook, who was already getting the food together, deigned to take notice of them. He emerged with three or four loaves of coarse, home-made bread which he handed first to father, then mother and then daughter.

As the sun rose and the light gradually improved, we saw the birds flashing over the horizon again: first a crested guan sailing high above the bay, followed by a pair of vivid blue humming birds, a blue tanager, a boat-tailed greckle and a black-and-yellow ora pendola. John jumped up and down with excitement when he spotted a keel-billed toucan, a rare bird that makes a strange, harsh, grating call.

Meanwhile more and more animals were arriving for breakfast. A troupe of about twenty coatis had turned up to see what was left from the tapirs' bread. Within half an hour, our acquaintances from the day before, the spider monkeys, arrived again. As usual the males came first, bent on filling their own stomachs before letting the other members of the family have a turn. The mothers trailed along behind with their babies clinging to their shoulders. A few older infants brought up the rear.

This time the spider monkeys showed off a wonderful tightrope act, swinging along the electricity wires that stretched from the roof of the cookhouse to a generator hidden far off in the forest. Once back in the trees, they moved from one branch to the next in a series of neatly timed swings ending in leaps, exactly like an acrobat on the trapeze. This way of getting around is known as brachiating and no one is as good at it as a spider monkey. They can swing through the trees faster than a man can walk along the forest floor, and jump over gaps of thirty feet or more.

The spider monkey has even more remarkable talents. It

can swing from a branch by its tail while it uses all four limbs to pluck fruit or to pick insects out of its hair. It has a fully prehensile tail, capable of supporting its entire weight for a long period. What an asset for an acrobat! If you look at the underside of this wonderful hand-tail, you will find a pad of naked skin, slightly ridged and whorled, like our own fingertips. This pad is so sensitive that it enables the spider monkey to pick up even very small objects, like berries, with its tail.

When the spider monkeys had passed, John and I found Mike propped up against a rock, apparently poking a huge pair of binoculars into a bush.

'This really must be a case of not seeing the wood for the trees,' John exclaimed as we walked up to him.

'Here, take a look for yourself,' Mike said, passing his field-glasses across to me. I took them up in a rather puzzled way but he gestured firmly at the leaf in front of him.

'There you are,' he said. 'Focus them at that.'

I suddenly realised that I was looking at a minute spider. Through the binoculars I could see something more remarkable – two even tinier flies, the size of midges, that appeared to have made their home upon its back. Through the binoculars they looked as big as bluebottles.

It was almost time for us to go back to the launch, since we were expected by some American friends who were running a tiny zoo on the mainland. But I felt I couldn't leave without visiting the baby spider monkey whose acquaintance I had made the evening before. He was the research station's only orphan. His mother had met a sad death after she had bitten a visitor who had approached too near and tried to stroke her baby. Since the mother was completely wild, her natural instinct was to use her teeth to protect her child from what she was bound to interpret as a hostile attack. The scientists did not know whether she had rabies or some other communicable disease and felt that their only option was to shoot her in order to run the tests.

So the baby was being brought up fitfully by a brilliant young girl researcher who was writing a thesis on spider monkeys. Unfortunately, the girl's enthusiasm for spider monkeys in practice seemed to be less than for her chosen subject in theory, and the baby appeared to be getting less attention than it needed. I was rather worried about it since it looked distinctly ill; its hair lacked gloss and was cold and matted, which is perhaps the most obvious sign of illness in an animal. I got a clue to what was wrong when the girl pulled a jug of milk out of a freezer in order to give the baby a meal. The milk was so cold that it had a thin skin of ice on top of it but without warming it up, she poured it into a bottle and simply passed it to the baby who promptly started to suck at it. But after a couple of gulps the baby turned its head away because the milk was so cold.

I felt rather humble about trying to advise a research scientist who was on the way to getting her doctorate but I felt obliged to point out that baby monkeys aren't really all that different to human babies. They both need affection and cuddling and warm milk. I hope that the Barro Colorado monkey has been getting all of them since. I am afraid that all the zoological learning in the world can't make up for the absence of affection and the mothering instinct.

Our first spider monkeys at Kilverstone came not from Panama but from Peru. The Jivaro Indians of northern Peru tell a delightful story to explain why the spider monkey has no thumbs. In contrast to its long agile tail, the spider monkey has hooks rather than hands – four claw-like fingers that are usually bunched tightly together.

According to the Peruvian fable, one day the spider monkey (called Maquisapa by the Jivaro Indians) met the howler monkey (or Coto) in the forest. The male howler monkey has a peculiarity of its own – a big bulge under its jaw the size and shape of a lemon. This is a voice-box that serves as an amplifier for the ear-splitting hurricane sounds that it makes to tell other howler monkeys who is the boss in its part of the forest.

According to the Indian story, the spider monkey found the howler monkey eating coconuts. 'Oh, that does look good!' exclaimed the spider monkey. 'Please, Coto, show me how to crack coconuts.'

The howler monkey obliged by pounding two coconuts together until one broke open. But when the spider monkey tried to copy him, his great, gangling arms made him clumsy and his elbows kept getting in the way. When he finally managed to bring two coconuts together, his thumbs got caught in between and were chopped off. While the spider monkey wailed and writhed about, the howler monkey roared with laughter.

Like the fox that lost its tail, the spider monkey resolved to get his revenge. 'Good morning, Coto,' he said next time they met beside the coconut tree. The howler monkey was pounding away at a coconut. 'I wouldn't bother to do that,' went on the spider monkey, 'I've discovered that coconuts taste much better if you swallow them just as they are.'

The simple-minded Coto believed the spider monkey and swallowed a coconut whole. It got stuck in his throat and he could not get it out. This, according to the Jivaro tribe, is why the descendants of the spider monkey have no thumbs, and why the Coto has a bulge in its throat.

Spider monkeys come in a baffling array of different colours. We bought two families to Kilverstone – Eric's family, who are completely black and have perpetually worried faces, and another family of silvery grey spider monkeys. Eric's lot have a nickname which they earned after a famous escape.

One night John had gone to a meeting and I was sitting alone by the fire. Suddenly there was a great stamping and clattering in the hall, punctuated by breathless squeaking noises. I thought for a moment that the peccaries had got loose and were stampeding up the stairs. Then I saw Valerie, the sweet, rotund girl who helps about the house, come heaving through the doorway, clad in dressing gown and bare feet.

'Milady, milady,' she panted, 'I've just seen a horrible great black man and he's trying to get into the house! I saw his black hand at the window!'

'Now, Valerie, calm down and tell me exactly what you saw.'

'Well, milady, first of all I heard a tapping at the window. I thought it might have been just a bird, or a bough scratching across the pane with the wind and all. But then I thought to myself, there isn't any wind. So it couldn't be that. Then I thought it must be John the butler playing a trick on me. He's a rogue, that one. He's often enough come up behind me and given me a good fright, he has. So I called out the window, "I know that's you out there, John. I'm on to your little tricks." Then I opened the window to give him a good ticking off. But as soon as I got the catch open, in came this long black hand. It scared me half to death.'

Valerie's imagination was in full spate. Gasping as if in fear of her life, she reminded me that there had been something in the newspaper about a black rapist. Then she remembered reading something else about the Black Hand Gang.

'Well, come on, we'd better go and see.'

We marched down to the staff-room. The room looked absolutely normal, with the television flickering away in the corner. The window was shut, as it had been after Valerie had slammed it in her fright. I opened it and up jumped a spider monkey. Valerie gasped and clamped her hand to her bosom, then, seeing what it was, gave an embarrassed giggle.

So we had one spider monkey back. But if he had got out, how many others had also escaped? As I shut the window, I thought I saw another shadow dart across the garden. It was almost pitch dark outside, with only a sliver of moon in the sky, so I got a torch to go out hunting.

I went wandering about outside, flashing the torch up into the trees and calling out idiotically, 'Where are you my baby, baby, babies?' I was counting on the fact that they had all got to know me well and might be lured out by the sound of my voice.

Brian, the curator, soon arrived with some of the keepers and we roamed about together, making what he thought were plausible spider monkey calls. One of the keepers said that he thought he had seen a monkey swinging about in an archway that we call Calcutta, known to the keepers, inevitably, as 'Oh Calcutta'.

Just as we received this intelligence, John got home from his meeting. We trooped over to the outbuildings and stables where the archway stands. There, sure enough, was Eric, swinging by his tail from a beam very high up inside the roof.

John hit on a plan of campaign at once. 'Rosamund, you get on with monkeys best. Why don't you get up on a ladder and lure the blighter down?'

I was not over-enthusiastic about this since I have never had much of a head for heights. I was even less enthusiastic when a great rickety ladder was produced that looked as if it might have been used by firemen trying to reach a blaze on the sixth floor.

I wobbled my way up the ladder towards Eric, who was now showing off his acrobatics by leaping from one beam to the next. 'Come on, Eric baby,' I kept cooing.

I was feeling wobbly enough as I got towards the top of the ladder, but it was nearly my downfall when Eric answered my calls by springing on to my head and shoulders. The ladder swayed giddily as Eric wound his tail tightly round my neck.

'If you make me climb a great big fireman's ladder,' I shouted to John, 'you might at least provide a safety net.'

But I got safely down. The next problem was what to do with Eric. John shooed us into the nearest room that he thought might be suitable. As it happened, it was the gun room – not quite the place to be with a wide-awake monkey acrobat. The room is full of glass cases containing stuffed birds and animals of every kind that had been shot at Kilverstone over the past century. Eric was delighted by his new surroundings. He leaped from one glass case to the next, trilling and gurgling his appreciation of every fellow creature that he came across. Brian and I had to dash back and forth, clutching at one case after another before it toppled and splintered into little bits. The tussle went on for what seemed like hours.

'Watch out for the white stoat!' Brian would yell. 'Quick, the golden pheasant!'

In the midst of all those glass cases there is a little stairway leading up to a sort of gallery that runs round the room higher up. When Eric tired of swinging back and forth between the glass cases, he darted up there. I followed him up, billing and cooing, and making 'huh huh' noises that I hoped would prove irresistible, trying to coax him back on to my head or shoulders. His response was not quite what I had wanted. He wrapped his arms and legs round me, but when I started to move downstairs he wrapped his terrible tail round the banisters and it stuck to the railing like glue. The same thing was repeated again and again.

Eric did not tire of the game until about three o'clock in the morning, by which time we were sitting about red-eyed, wondering whether to leave the white stoat and golden pheasant to their fate and return to do battle in the morning. But Eric finally decided he had had enough and deigned to accept a ride on my shoulders.

We had had to switch off all the lights in the outbuildings, since we knew that the glow of a light bulb would draw the monkey unerringly back towards it. We were marching up the drive towards the house when we noticed that someone had forgotten to switch off one of the lights in the stables. Eric noticed it too, and I felt him brace himself for a leap from my shoulders back towards the light. I grabbed his feet, determined not to go through another four hours of monkey-catching before breakfast. Eric was infuriated by the interference and started biting and scraping at me with his tough little claws.

'For God's sake let him go,' Brian urged.

I needed no persuasion after a sudden nip that made me feel that I had just lost my right ear lobe. I let go and Eric shot off towards the stables but instead of going inside, he darted up on to the roof, over the crest of the gable and on to the flat bit beyond which extends over the garage where some of the keepers have a flat. We were still stumbling about by the dying light of our torches when a whoop of delight went up from keepers Geoffrey and Stuart. They had found Eric in the flat's boxroom, where the jumble of assorted bric-à-brac had proved irresistible to the monkey's curiosity. They managed to shut the door and the windows before he could do another bolt. The boxroom contained a marvellous battered old tin trunk of the sort used for carting all your worldly possessions by ship from one side of the globe to the other. We wrapped Eric up in a bedspread and locked him up inside the trunk.

Trudging back to the house with the tin trunk, I suddenly remembered that I had left the other monkey in Valerie's room. He had been living up to his name of spider monkey. He had strung Valerie's knitting from every corner in sight, making the whole room look as if an enormous spider had spun a web across it. As he hopped across the floor on all fours with his elbows and knees sticking up, he looked uncannily like a spider himself. We popped him into the trunk with Eric and back they went to the cage. But Valerie in her excitement had already given them the nickname by which they would be known throughout the park – the Black Hand Gang.

5

Sex with the Miniature Horses

I grew up amongst horses and have always loved riding. But I must admit I had been spoiled. When I was a child we had a wonderful groom so I had never learned to saddle or bridle a horse. I had never had to muck out stables. And I knew little more than the average motorist about horses' sex life. A child who belongs to a pony club today probably knows a good deal more than I did.

You might wonder what horses are doing in a South American zoo. The horse is not a native of South America but a modern import from the Old World. The triumphs of the Spanish conquistadores owed a great deal to the astonishment of the Aztecs and the Incas confronted with their unknown beasts. But in the centuries since Cortés and Pizarro a unique breed of horses has been developed in Argentina.

The Falabellas of Argentina are the smallest horses in the world. The tiniest of them stand no more than fifteen or sixteen inches high when young – smaller than a labrador. Yet they are perfectly proportioned and for this reason should never be compared with the Shetland pony. The Shetland looks altogether different from a normal-sized horse: very stocky, with short, stumpy legs and an over-sized head and body. Falabellas are thoroughbreds in miniature and look like perfect scale models of familiar breeds. You can find Falabellas that look exactly like thoroughbred race-horses, seen through the wrong end of a telescope. They come in all colours and there are spotted ones, too. Unlike most normal horses, however, Falabellas can live as long as fifty years and Falabella mares can still foal at the age of forty. They have two ribs fewer – and two vertebrae fewer – than other horses and take slightly longer to foal: nearer thirteen months rather than the usual eleven months.

From the moment I first read about the Falabellas, I was determined to find some for Kilverstone. How this extra-ordinary breed had come to exist at all was a mysterious – even a romantic – question. I collected half a dozen stories about the origins of the Falabellas, each more colourful than the last, before the first of them arrived at the park. Many of the stories – like the one in the *Guinness Book of Records* – revolved around the idea that normal horses had been trapped in the barren, windswept terrain of Patagonia, perhaps by a landslide in a solitary canyon. There was little to eat except cactus so the smallest horses had the best chance of survival. The surviving offspring of the original horses grew smaller and smaller until they became recognisable as the Falabellas of today. This theory was given support by published accounts of the case of some Hereford cattle that strayed into a valley in the Rockies and were cut off. Some years later their offspring were found to have shrunk to half the original size. The explanation was held to lie in the absence of minerals vital to growth processes in the soil and vegetation of the area.

I heard more fanciful tales. For example, one of the Argentine dealers whom we had met told us that the founder of the Falabella strain learned the secrets of how to breed tiny horses from the chief of the Cayak Indians. A romantic but unlikely story – after all, why should Amerindians breed miniature horses? It has even been suggested that Japanese immigrant workers in Argentina, skilled in the arts of producing miniature trees, had somehow managed to apply their science to horses.

I heard yet another account: that in the last century the grand old man of the Falabella family sent some of his thoroughbreds down to Patagonia and then forgot about them. Two generations later, his grandchildren remembered his legacy, sent home some of their gauchos to find out what had happened to the horses and discovered that they had shrunk to a fraction of the original size.

My heart was set on bringing a herd of Falabellas to Kilverstone. But the first little horses I was able to find were not Falabellas, but miniature horses of a kind that had been bred in Europe since the sixteenth century and were popular as a status symbol at the courts of Europe in the time of Louis XIV. While the Falabellas were generally believed to have originated through an accident of nature, the miniature horses were bred to be small through generations of selective care.

We found that our first miniature horses at Kilverstone even depended on us for their sex life. Three miniature horses – a little black stallion called Piccolo and two mares that we called Evita and Anabella – had just arrived. We had fenced off the lawn between the house and the stables, dotted with mulberry and apple trees, into six little paddocks. We could move the horses from one to another to ensure that they had a steady supply of grass.

I had blithely assumed that mating was something that could be left to them but things were not that simple.

To begin with, Evita and Anabella came into season at the same time. Piccolo was torn between two ardent women. If he responded to Evita's advances, Anabella would canter up like a jealous wife and deliver a powerful kick. If he tried to appease Anabella, it would be Evita's turn to whinny and kick. The mare who was currently receiving Piccolo's attentions would further provoke the other by prancing about in a very skittish style. Evita, in particular, lived up to her name by acting the complete coquette.

The eternal triangle is not all that much fun if its dramas are played out in the same paddock. We decided that the only answer was to offer Evita another stallion so that both mares would be satisfied. So we brought in Humbug, black and white with a very sweet disposition, who became a great favourite with the children, and parcelled him off to one of the paddocks with Evita. Now, I thought, the problem was solved. Our two happily married couples would get on with the job and Kilverstone would soon be celebrating the arrival of its first miniature foals. I was wrong again.

The mares were soon in season again and Piccolo and Humbug prepared to fulfil their marital duties. But each time they tried to mount their respective partners, all they managed to do was to shunt them around the paddocks like wheelbarrows. After a few minutes of this they would flop down to the ground, seemingly exhausted. When they recovered their strength, instead of returning to their unfinished business, Humbug and Piccolo would puff themselves up, strut about the lawn and start neighing at each other across the paddock which had been left empty in between. No doubt they were bragging about what prize studs they were or casting aspersions on each other's virility! Eventually, when they tired of showing off, they would return to their wheelbarrow race, which would end exactly as before.

'Just like men,' I said to John. 'The ones who talk loudest are never up to much.'

We could not understand what had gone wrong. We called on a friend who had some experience of horses for advice.

'I don't know how they manage it in the wild,' she said. 'They never seem to be able to manage much in captivity without getting humans involved in the act.'

She was not exaggerating. Indeed, with the help of Humbug and a more experienced mare called Florence, she treated us to a practical demonstration. She did just about everything for Humbug that had to be done, short of taking his place. She held the mare's tail out of the way, kept a steady grip on her so that she would not buck or kick, kept Humbug pointed in the right direction and gave him a few encouraging pats and shoves.

'There,' said our friend after what seemed to have been a satisfactory performance. 'Now you know what to do.'

'Will we really have to go through all that?' asked John uncertainly.

'I'm afraid the answer is basically yes. But you may find that their aim improves with practice.'

'My God, I hope so.'

'How often should they do it?' I ventured, trying to be practical.

'Well, you'll have to play it by ear. But if you want to take advantage of the mares' season, you should probably keep them at it several times a day.'

So when Evita and Anabella came on heat again we knew what we were required to do. We got Piccolo comfortably dossed down in his own lust-hutch, an airy stable with plenty of hay and oats to keep up his amorous energies. Every three or four hours we would bring in one or other of the mares and help Piccolo do his stuff exactly as we had been instructed. This went on for two days. I don't know whether the pace was killing for Piccolo but it certainly was for us.

In between these bouts in the hay, John would go back to the park to work on some cages he was building. I would trot down every few hours to fetch him. 'Come on, darling,' I would say. 'Piccolo's due for his oats.'

By the third morning I was completely shattered. It was then I committed a terrible faux pas. I didn't feel strong enough to walk across the walled garden so I called over to John, 'Darling, let's go and mate again. It's at least three hours since we did it last.'

There was a great 'harrumph' from just behind me, and I spun round to see a very prim schoolmistress flanked by a bevy of small boys and girls who could have walked straight out of St Trinian's. If she could have put her fingers in all their ears at once, I do believe she would have done it. '*Please*,' she said severely. 'Not in front of the children.'

This made me realise what I had let slip. I blushed to the roots of my hair and beat a hasty retreat, gasping apologetically, 'Horses, it's only horses.' This did not seem to appease the schoolmarm – she rather looked as if she thought the explanation made it worse.

Our efforts as sexual tutors to the little horses did succeed in increasing their enthusiasm for the mating game. Once they began to master the art, it seemed they could never get enough of it. We were invited up to the BBC studios in Birmingham to do a live programme on Kilverstone. The producers especially wanted us to bring the little horses so Piccolo, Evita and Anabella all made their debuts in a television studio.

They were as obedient as gun-dogs throughout the programme. But as we headed out of the studio and down a long, glass-walled corridor overlooking a courtyard, Piccolo smelled spring in the air and tried to mount Evita. I had a sudden vision of the bill for smashing a hundred feet or so of plate glass. With the help of Geoffrey, their keeper who had accompanied us, I managed to separate them and get them outside and on to the pavement.

There, as the studio audience – mostly women but including a particularly inscrutable Chinaman – filtered down the steps, Piccolo tried again to show them that he had learned his lessons.

The ladies took it all in good humour but the Chinaman seemed mystified. 'What's happening? What is he doing?' he demanded.

When I explained, he seemed even more worried.

Geoffrey intervened to pull Piccolo away but Piccolo was less than amused at this rude interference and started having a go at Geoffrey too.

The Chinaman looked thunderstruck. 'What's he doing now?'

I was too embarrassed to explain. I don't suppose it's allowed in China.

6

By Paddle down
the Amazon

Our labours seemed to be starting to pay off towards the
end of the second year, when the number of visitors to
Kilverstone at last reached 60,000. But we were still a long
way from that crucial 100,000. We could comfort ourselves
with the thought that it was only a couple of years since
we had driven in the first nail and turned the first sod, but
there was that yawning gap on the balance sheet between
our earnings and our outgoings. At least the bank manager
still smiled. I suppose he had reason to; after all, he was
collecting his fifteen per cent interest on the overdraft.
For John there was the headache of wondering how to
pay the bills during the next long, barren winter that
lay ahead.

I had new worries, too. There was a new jungle baby in
the house who needed attention – Pinchit, the baby
capuchin monkey. At the same time I had lost (at least
temporarily) one of my own children. My eldest son, Jamie,
had heard all about our first expeditions to South America
and had caught the bug. He had just qualified as a chartered
accountant but felt that before he got tied down to a City
desk he should go out and see something of the world.

Jamie talked of buying a small yacht and sailing it across the Atlantic to Latin America. 'Then I want to get into the jungle,' he said. 'I've read that it's possible to sail right down the Amazon in a canoe.' He talked of visiting the Indian settlements along the borders of Peru and Brazil and buying up animals for Kilverstone. 'Better still,' he said, 'I'll try to bag you a black jaguar.'

That was an exciting idea. The rare and mysterious black jaguar is rarely seen in captivity. We had heard in Iquitos that black jaguars had been sighted from light planes in the river valleys along the Brazilian border. So my nervousness about Jamie heading off on his romantic and dangerous expedition was mixed with the hope that he would actually succeed in finding us one of the elusive animals.

But he had to become a yachtsman before trying his hand as a canoeist and animal-trapper. With two friends, Jamie bought a boat called the *Imagine*. It looked absurdly small and frail as I watched them putting out from Southampton. None of the boys had ever sailed the open sea before but Jamie has a knack of handling rough situations in his quiet way. At any rate, there was no need to worry about his fortunes on the voyage. Stopping over in Gibraltar for repairs, the boys sailed the *Imagine* to Antigua, making the crossing in record time – not bad going for accountancy students turned amateur seamen. John and I flew out to Tobago to rendezvous with Jamie there, and spent a glorious idle week of calypso, rum punches, and bathing in a palm-ringed horseshoe bay that had once been a pirate cove.

The boys sailed on through the West Indies and along the coasts of Venezuela and Colombia up to the San Blase islands off the coast of Panama. At this point Jamie's friends decided it was time to move on. They sailed to Fort Lauderdale in Florida, where they managed to sell the boat and earned some pocket-money by working as 'English butlers' – which are all the rage in America – at a couple of local society parties. For Jamie the adventure had barely begun. He had stuck to his plan to sail the headwaters of the Amazon alone in a native canoe. As he put it, 'I wanted to test myself out.'

When I thought about it again, I realised just how risky his plan might prove to be. The Amazon is not just a river: it is a wilderness of water with its springs in the Andean snows, covering half the land surface of Brazil and bits of another eight Latin American countries with a labyrinth of rivers, swamps and rainforests. The Amazon basin is believed to contain two-thirds of the river water in the entire world. It also contains piranhas, enormous snakes, headhunters and giant spiders. It breeds deadly fevers and gut-rotting diseases and offers less well-known but even nastier hazards, like the tiny barbed fish called the candiru, which can lodge itself in the apertures of the body and has to be cut out in a messy operation that I would not like to have to undergo on a remote riverbank among the caymans and giant catfish.

Jamie telephoned me from Lima to say he was ready to set off along the Inca trail to the Amazon. I couldn't disguise the uncertainty in my voice. Jamie then said that if I was going to be terribly upset by his plan to paddle alone by native canoe, he would abandon it. I promptly said, 'Go ahead'. I reflected that I had never done as much as I had wanted entirely on my own, but that I had derived immense satisfaction from what I had managed to do by myself. I avoided telling Jamie the story that I suddenly remembered having been told in Iquitos. It was about the British Consul there, who was frequently approached by museums and research institutes that were trying to acquire shrunken heads from the warlike Indians north of the Rio Negro. One day the Consul set off to make contact with a tribe of headhunters that helped him to satisfy the museums. He was told that he was in luck that day. The headhunters could offer *una cosa especial*, 'something rather special'. It turned out to be the head of a French trader who had lived in Iquitos and was something of a local celebrity, known to all and sundry as 'Vive la France'. Even reduced to the size of a cricket ball, the Frenchman's face was unmistakable from the flaming red hair and blue eyes. 'Vive la France' had staggered off into the jungle on a blind drunk once too often.

Jamie had flown to Lima from Fort Lauderdale, where the boys had sold the boat and gone their separate ways. He now set off on foot along the Inca trail – not for him the relative comforts of the picturesque, snaking trans-Andean railway that John and I had used to reach the Amazonian hinterlands of Peru. Jamie slept by night in whatever shelter he could find, wrapped in an Indian poncho. Beyond the ruined Inca terraces of Machu Picchu, a haunting sight through the mountain mists at first light, Jamie spent one night in a cave at least 13,000 feet above sea level. He had supped on tinned sardines and he woke to find an agouti snuffling beside his head. We were fascinated to hear that the agouti, which is usually to be found scuttling along through the jungle undergrowth, will also venture so high up into the bitter cold of the Andes. The agouti is probably the most hunted animal in Latin America, a popular source of protein for man and jaguar alike. Normally it is a daylight feeder, but it must have found the fishy smells irresistible.

Coming down through the Andean foothills, Jamie walked on into the jungle, where he spent a couple of nights with a strange Austrian squatter who had fled civilisation – and his wife – to live in an isolated shack and farm a few acres he had hacked from the jungle.

Jamie decided that he would sail down the Madre de Dios, one of the smaller tributaries of the Amazon that flows from Peru into Brazil. He bought a native canoe and worked to get it shipshape. He painted the canoe in the Clifford colours as a tribute to George Clifford, third Earl of Cumberland, a swashbuckling ancestor who was a favourite of Queen Elizabeth I and a bit of a pirate. Cumberland had sailed the Caribbean and had taken San José in Puerto Rico, which Drake had tried and failed several times to capture.

The Madre de Dios is about half a mile wide, and Jamie steered his canoe close to the far bank, where the current ran fastest. Setting out at first light, he would be sailing in the shade, but by 8.30 or 9 the sun was blazing directly overhead. It was just after the rainy season and the river was swirling with dead trees and debris, a thick, murky colour. There was no chance of catching a cat-nap without running into flotsam.

Sailing downriver was like riding through a tunnel with a narrow slit open overhead. The trees shot straight up for 100 feet or more on either side. The jungle was so thick that the vegetation beyond the first line of trees was an impenetrable black net; to walk for five or ten minutes inland would have been to be lost for ever.

The journey was punctuated by the raucous screech of parrots and macaws, which would shoot across the narrow slit of sky every twenty minutes or so and be lost to sight. Along the river bank, Jamie saw hundreds of small white birds, egrets or herons.

Jamie went swimming whenever he felt like it. He was not frightened of piranhas because the water was running high and because, contrary to popular belief, piranhas will rarely attack a human who is moving about in the water unless the river is low and they are short of food. There are 5,000 different varieties of fish in the Amazon basin, compared with 1,500 in the Congo and only 150-odd in Europe. But local fishermen whom Jamie met complained that the fish population on the Madre de Dios had been declining since the introduction of insecticides.

The frustration of the rainforest is that you hear many more creatures than you ever manage to see. Throughout the voyage, Jamie heard the echoing boom of the howler monkeys but saw only one towards the end of the voyage. After he heard a jaguar roar nearby, he took to spending the nights on the islands along the river.

One reason why he did not try to travel at night, apart from the risk of a collision with a hurtling log, was that the giant anacondas have a habit of floating down behind a log – or a canoe – and flipping themselves on to it in order to hitch a ride.

Unfortunately, Jamie had eaten his last supper in town in Puerto Maldonado, the capital of Madre de Dios province in Peru. He ate in a communal restaurant, frequented by seven or eight local families. The dish of the day was stewed margay. By the end of the first day on the river he was already feeling sick, although he put this down at first to sunstroke from the sun beating down relentlessly through the hollow tunnel of the trees.

By the third morning, Jamie was very weak and had great difficulty in hauling his canoe back into the water. The river was falling amazingly fast and he found the boat, which he had left at the water's edge the night before, stranded high up on a sandbank. The canoe, by the way, was no balsa-wood contraption but a twenty-foot-long, hollowed-out tree-trunk. With the aid of a makeshift lever, Jamie finally eased the canoe down into the water.

But within an hour or so there was one of those sudden tropical rains for which the Amazon is notorious, gunning down from directly overhead like machine-gun fire, with such force that it stirred up waves. With his fever raging, Jamie suddenly felt icy-cold. He made for an island further downstream, where he found a wooden-frame hut thatched with reeds. Inside there were dry logs with which he could make a fire – what a windfall!

He managed to dry out that night, at the cost of scorching his poncho in front of the fire. He was still convinced that there could not be anything seriously wrong with him and was determined to press on. He carried on downriver for another day until he came to a large, hauntingly beautiful island with a wide, sandy beach along its eastern side. It was like a dream in the midst of all that mud and silt. The sand was fringed by reeds and bamboo-like plants which Jamie was able to chop down to make tripod stands from which to sling his hammock. His hammock looked like a tent suspended above the ground; it had a waterproof roof and mosquito netting along the side – something the early rubber-tappers would have given their eye-teeth to have had.

Come the morning, Jamie found that the river had risen again as fast as it had sunk the day before. The water was lapping over the tripod stands of his hammock. By the time he had moved the hammock and rigged up palm fronds overhead to provide extra shade, he felt utterly played out. He finally took his temperature with a thermometer that I had taken the precaution of giving him in Tobago. When he saw that it was 107°, he decided, as he later told me, 'that I had better be fairly sensible'. He decided to spend a couple of days resting up on the island.

That evening he was awakened by the whirring sound of an outboard engine. A dugout canoe was passing, carrying Brazil nuts down river. The two men on the canoe stopped and asked Jamie whether they could stay with him on the island overnight. They told him they were cooking *sopa de mono* – monkey soup – for supper and offered him some to try. As the darkness fell and they all sat round the camp fire eating the soup, Jamie saw one of the men pull out a small round object from the bowl and start to crunch it up in his teeth. It was the head of a marmoset or tamarin.

The next morning the monkey soup men moved on, waving and joking. Jamie weakly prepared to follow suit. Paddling along slowly, he managed to make it to the border post at the Bolivian frontier, where he found an army patrol in a little tin shack and a straggle of mud huts thatched with palm. The soldiers were anxious to help, but in their kindness they put Jamie into the tin hut, where the temperature was about 120°F. When he felt a little stronger, he crawled into the cool under the floor of the hut.

I think Jamie's life was saved by a fat, swarthy little Catholic priest called Father Carlos who appeared a few days after he reached the border post. He took one look at Jamie, muttered 'Muy malo, muy malo,' and rigged up a bit of rubber tubing from a nail in a tree. He proceeded to feed Jamie an intravenous drip into a hole he punctured in his arm. I imagine that what was in the tube was mostly glucose, which Jamie certainly needed. By the time the priest came again to give him the treatment for a second time, he had not eaten for about sixteen days.

'Te necesita una mujer,' Father Carlos told him on his return visit. 'What you need is a woman.'

Jamie smiled weakly and said that, unfortunately, that was about the last thing he could manage just then. It seemed an odd prescription from a priest but then, jungle priests are certainly different.

'Yo soy catolico peruviano,' Father Carlos explained. 'I am a Peruvian Catholic, not Roman Catholic.' Jamie discovered that Father Carlos had an Indian 'wife' and four children. He practised what he preached.

Jamie was still determined to carry on so the border guards dolled him up in a bush hat with a flap of linen hanging down over his neck and made him take a parasol as well. He headed downstream for an hour or two, and then collapsed again. He struggled back to the border post, realising that he would have to abandon the expedition. Some Indians at the post asked him about the journey and, hearing about the island where he had rested up, exclaimed that it was haunted and that that must be the origin of his sickness. They said that the only way to cure him was to wrap him up in tobacco leaves. Jamie declined the offer, thinking that he would never be able to pay for enough tobacco leaves to cover all 6'3" of him.

He got a lift on an army launch back to Puerto Maldonado, flew to Cuzco on a flight on which three of the plane's four engines conked out, took another flight to Lima and finally got on board a plane back to England.

'Sorry I didn't get that black jaguar,' Jamie croaked, He looked like a Buchenwald survivor. I packed him off to the Hospital for Tropical Diseases, and it took over three months to produce a firm diagnosis of what was wrong with him. He had picked up a form of blood poisoning called toxoplasmosis from eating that margay stew in Puerto Maldonado. It was months before we got him looking like something livelier than a skeleton and a whole year before he was fully recovered.

So we didn't get our black jaguar. But the Austrian friend Jamie had made in the Peruvian jungle sounded like a perfect contact for Kilverstone wildlife park. A keen sailor who had been to school in Hampstead, he had become a devotee of the jungle, forsaking everything in order to live in it. He kept only one link to the outside world – a very sophisticated radio capable of picking up any waveband, on which he would settle down among the mosquitoes to listen to the news in Chinese, German, French or English. He was devoted to the Indian tribes of his area and had paid out of his own pocket for an inoculation programme that had successfully eradicated malaria amongst the tribes with which he was in contact. He had a margay trained as a pet which one of the Indians had given to him as a gesture of thanks. He offered to help to get any animals we wanted from his Indian friends. Alas, when John and I returned to Peru the following year, he had vanished into deep jungle on one of his long, solitary safaris.

7

Monkey Business

When I brought an emaciated Jamie home to Kilverstone, he found himself in a monkey house. Charlie, the tamarin, had been exiled to a cage but the capuchins had moved in. The capuchins are the most intelligent of the South American monkeys. In their quickness and imagination they are often a match even for the African ape. They have relatively large, highly convoluted brains rather like our own, which may explain the speed with which they learn to use simple tools. They get their name from the way their colouring resembles the habit of the Capuchin monk. It took no time at all for our capuchins at Kilverstone to master simple techniques like unscrewing a lid from a jar, which they learned to do much faster than I can. They also learnt to fasten and unfasten bolts so we always had to keep their cages padlocked. At an American zoo, they tried out the simple experiment of offering capuchins a mouse on a string in order to gather food that had been left beyond their reach. After only a brief trial, the monkeys were able to direct the mouse and collect the food.

Some remarkable stories are told about the capacities of trained capuchins. In his book, *The Monkey Kingdom*, Ivan Sanderson recalls the remarkable feats of a capuchin who travelled the New England coast of America with her owner, an organ-grinder, for several summers after the War.

She not only passed the hat around after the music was played but was capable of distinguishing how much each member of the audience had given and of making the appropriate response. If a dime, a quarter or a banknote was offered, she would take it courteously and doff her hat with great solemnity, putting the money in one of two special compartments in her owner's wallet. If she was offered a nickel, she would take it, put it in yet another compartment of the wallet and casually touch her hat. If a penny or a metal token without any value was offered, she would examine it carefully and then throw it to the ground contemptuously, chattering all the while. If she approached a member of the audience who gave her nothing, she would stand there and scream and scream in a fashion that seemed to be designed to create maximum embarrassment in the unfortunate victim.

We bought two white-fronted capuchins whom we soon christened Snatch and Grab because of their appalling table manners. A visitor who strayed too close to their cage would risk losing anything that could be snatched away from him – cigarette, spectacles or even handbag. When people disobeyed our signs and tried to feed them, as unfortunately so many thoughtless visitors to zoos will always do, Snatch would insist on keeping his mate in her place. He would grab everything that was going and harry her back into the far corner of the cage.

We soon found that Grab was not an ideal mother. When she killed her first baby, we made excuses for her, arguing that this was the first time she had given birth, that she had been in great pain and may, in a sense, have been trying to get her own back for something she could not properly understand. But when she threw her second baby away the night it was born, causing it to die before we could do anything to save it, we became extremely alarmed. Puzzled to find an explanation for her behaviour, we became convinced that the capuchins just did not like babies. If they saw a child holding a doll or a teddy bear they would become very excited, rattling the bars of their cage, grimacing and screeching. They did not mind a human baby – that was too big for them to think of as a baby monkey. As Grab was continually being beaten up by her husband, Snatch, maybe she was taking it out on the babies, as I'm told sometimes happens in human families.

We had learnt caution by the time Grab gave birth to her third baby. We kept watch on the capuchins' cage right round the clock. During the first week after birth, Grab tended her baby like a normal mother. We began to relax a little, hoping that everything would turn out all right after all. Then one family that had been visiting the cage rushed to tell the keepers that something very nasty was happening. They said that Grab had been trying to stuff her baby into a hole in the ground under a log, apparently trying to bury it alive. Stuart, the monkey keeper, rushed to the cage, took Snatch away and locked him up in another cage. Then he went in and rescued the baby.

After this I decided I would have to raise the baby myself if it was to stand any chance of surviving. It was a tiny, bedraggled little thing, very battered and frail. My first instinct was to stuff it inside my jumper, to keep it warm from my own body heat and also because I thought that the beating of my heart would console it and make it feel safe, rather as if it was next to its own mother's breast. This was rather short-sighted on my part. Inevitably, the baby capuchin, which I had already decided to call Pinchit, made a mess inside my jumper. I would have to treat it exactly like a human baby and make it wear a nappy.

This change of attire fascinated small children who visited the park. A few days later I was approached by an earnest young man about four years old, who demanded an explanation. I spun him a great story about how difficult it was to put a nappy on to a wriggling baby monkey. He told me very severely that I was wrong – it was not difficult at all. What you have to do, he said, is to hold the tail up and wrap the nappy round it, being careful not to stick the safety pin through it. He said he had often seen this done with his own baby brother. I tried to explain to him that Pinchit's tail might just be a trifle longer than what he was describing as his little brother's tail.

Pinchit had to be fed every three hours throughout the night as well as the day. The first night I had him in the house, I was frightened that I would not wake up to give him his regular feeds. I stayed up with him watching television, which seemed to excite him greatly, until fairly late. I then decided to play it safe and call the telephone exchange in order to book alarm calls for midnight, 3 a.m. and 6 a.m. The man on the exchange exclaimed in his broad Norfolk drawl, 'You must be mad.'

I couldn't find anything to say except 'Yes.' I didn't have the courage to explain to him why I wanted to be woken up every three hours. Perhaps that would only have made him conclude that I was even madder than I sounded.

One blessing about baby monkeys by comparison with their human cousins is that they don't cry. In most other respects they are pretty similar. There are the same problems of bottle-feeding and nappy-changing. I was worn out after three months when I was able to drop the night-time feeding and just feed Pinchit during the day. Even then, I still had to take him everywhere with me, to ensure that he did not miss his tucker.

When he was not on the bottle, Pinchit would spend most of his time sucking his thumb or even his big toes. He rode all the way from Kilverstone to London in the car sucking alternately the big toe of one foot and then the other. I started out by feeding him with a pen-dropper because his mouth was too tiny to cope with even the smallest baby bottle that we could buy in Thetford. Feeding became a little simpler when we were able to move him on to a specially made premature baby's bottle.

About a month before Pinchit was born, my chihuahua bitch, Tia, had given birth to puppies. In the small hours of the morning, waking up to give Pinchit his nightly feeds, I was often tempted to put him in with Tia's litter and hope that she would take care of him too. Since he had a very full set of pointed teeth, I thought this might be rather unfair on the dog. But Pinchit grew up amongst the puppies, and it sometimes seemed that he had come to think of himself as a chihuahua too. They all romped about the house together and became quite inseparable.

Walking about with a monkey inside your clothes every day presents certain hazards. One day I was gardening with Pinchit bobbing about inside my woolly jumper and Brian Dickson, the curator, came up and said, 'I don't know what the public must think, seeing your right bosom bouncing about all over the place.'

Pinchit graduated from nappies when he was three months old because John and I had to fly off to Madrid to look at animals in some collections there. Pinchit was left in the charge of Brian and my son, Charles. They wrestled with him for an entire hour, trying to get his nappy on, and finally gave up. For the whole week Pinchit roamed about without his nether garments. When we got back we found he had got to like his new freedom. When I tried to put a nappy back on him he wriggled out of it like a woman getting out of a girdle. We had to accept that he had come of age.

The easiest time in handling a baby monkey is the same as with a child; it is the stage when they cannot move about much, but lie still most of the day in a cot or basket or pram. As he got older, Pinchit developed an insatiable curiosity. Once he grabbed a cigarette from a guest and stuck it in his mouth. Sceptical about whether human beings could really enjoy such objects, he removed it from his mouth, stared at it quizzically and then popped it back in the other way round. The stages of his gradual coming of age were clearly defined. He reached the point when he would start pulling himself up in his basket and peering about the outside world, just like a baby in its pram. Then he would be able to haul himself out of his basket and crawl about. Finally, he was toddling around. From that time on, we were in for trouble.

As Pinchit tottered about on his first travels, Brian produced for me an object that we called the meat safe, a wire cage that we could put down over his basket when we wanted to keep him in one place. But we never used the meat safe on long trips in the car, when Pinchit enjoyed lots of cuddling. It was not long before he started treating the inside of the car as a sort of adventure playground. The steering wheel, in particular, he seemed to regard as a special climbing frame designed for a baby monkey, and would swing back and forth from it. This tended not to improve John's temper in a traffic jam.

In any case, as Pinchit grew bigger the meat safe was obviously too constricting for him. I found him a huge macaw cage, shaped rather like a mosque and gilded to boot – if you have to live in a cage, it should at least be a gilded one! We put ropes and perches inside for him to swing on like a miniature acrobat. Pinchit would swing back and forth and do somersaults in his cage and watch television in the library, while we would spend less of our time watching the programme than we did watching him.

Pinchit was growing up in more ways than one. Not long after our return from Madrid, I had to give a tea for the lady-helpers of a local charity. One of them was in the midst of a long dissertation on the perils of sex education in schools when her cup descended with a resounding clang into her saucer. She broke off in midstream and stared fixedly at Pinchit who returned her gaze. That wasn't all he was doing. With no embarrassment at all, he was doing publicly what many adolescent boys do furtively.

It was too much for my lady volunteer. 'I never thought

I would see anything like that in the sitting room!' she exploded.

One of the younger women snorted and erupted into little giggling fits, sounding exactly like one of those Hong Kong dolls that squeal with laughter when you pull a string.

Pinchit wasn't yet ready for a mate but he was obviously getting the right ideas. Of course, anyone who runs a wildlife park knows that the very best crowd binder you can have is a randy monkey, or preferably a pair or more of them. People who would never dream of attending a live sex show throng to the monkey cage to see our little cousins performing the same way – or at any rate doing their version of the same thing.

I couldn't resist asking Brian how he thought Pinchit had picked up the habit. He asked, with a twinkle in his eye, 'What would you say if I said that I had been giving him practical lessons myself?'

You can't run a zoo without a sense of humour!

By the time Pinchit was nine months old his mother was just about ready to give birth to yet another baby. She was able to produce them with clockwork regularity but never came to accept them as her own. I was not over-anxious to have a second baby monkey in the house, especially since I knew that at least five more baby monkeys were likely to be produced about the same time in the park.

I thought that I had better begin to get Pinchit accustomed to being with other monkeys as a preliminary to his re-entry into the park. He had started out thinking he was a chihuahua: now that he was flirting with our female visitors, my daughter, Trina, and my two step-daughters, it was beginning to look as if he had come to consider himself one of the family. We had no other little capuchins of his age, and although there were some spider monkeys who were only a few months older than he, they were more than twice his size. Still, they seemed to be the best available playmates.

I took him down to the spider monkeys' big cage every day and would sit there with him for an hour or so, hoping that they would begin to play together. The female spider monkey was called Misty, the male, Aztec. Pinchit liked to stay on my head when we visited them and there was one very sound reason for him to do this. Misty, although very sociable and chatty, was a little over-powerful. She packed a real punch and could knock little Pinchit across the cage like a ball of cotton wool. The only time Pinchit really gained confidence in her presence was when a group of us – Trina, little Pandora and I – came down to the spider monkeys' cage with him. He then plucked up enough courage to go scrambling up a tree at the back of the spider monkeys' cage. But as soon as Misty took a playful swipe at his tail to pull him down to the ground again, he came scampering back to the safety of his foster mother.

Just before Pinchit was finally exiled to the monkey house, I was staying with Trina for a couple of days in her Kensington house. We had just sat down to get our breath back after a shopping expedition when Trina said that she was expecting an Italian girl friend who was bringing along an Italian man whom I had not met before. When the doorbell rang, Pinchit was sitting on my head and had got his hands inextricably entangled in my hair. I tried desperately to get him off before the guests arrived but he held on tight and I realised that I could only remove him if I was prepared to lose a fistful of hair. So I sat tight.

The Italian man was almost a parody of continental manners. He ignored the monkey on my head and proceeded to kiss my hand and make light conversation. It was only an hour or so later, as he prepared to leave, that he remarked on how he had always been fascinated by monkeys. He behaved as if it were the most normal thing in the world to walk into a house in London and find a friend's mother sitting with a monkey in her hair. Fortunately, Trina had long since given up apologising for her eccentric mother.

Having accustomed him to company by letting him play with the spider monkeys, we felt that Pinchit was ready to take up residence in a cage of his own next to his parents in the monkey house. It was just as well, since Snatch and Grab's new baby had just arrived. I was worried that this one would not last long if we left it with them, so when it was just six days old I whisked if off to the house. I decided to call the new baby capuchin Nickit, since we had learned something by then about the kleptomaniac tendencies of the species.

We were due to travel down to a zoological conference near my brother's home at Ugbrooke in Devon the day I took Nickit into the house. Armed with plenty of nappies and baby bottles, we set off. Everyone at the conference was very tolerant, considering the circumstances. We arrived a bit late and had to sit in the front row. The time for Nickit's feed and change of nappies came well before the session ended. This was probably good for the meeting: you can't be too pompous about chairing a conference if you can see a baby monkey having a nappy changed right under your nose.

'All babies are the same, aren't they?' whispered an old dear in the row behind us. Maybe it was a useful reminder of what zoos are all about.

When we got Nickit home we quickly fell into the same routine as with Pinchit. He needed to be fed about once every three hours, day or night. Tia the chihuahua quickly took him in hand. Tia had had a puppy called Pedro not long before and they became the greatest of friends. They shared a basket and would sleep together and romp around in it. When Nickit grew a little bigger he graduated to the gilt cage that Pinchit had occupied before. Like Pinchit he was an avid viewer of television – especially the 'Survival' and 'Vanishing World' programmes.

Monkeys, even if born of the same parents, are as different from each other as are human brothers and sisters. Pinchit had been a great jumper and leaper but Nickit had sloth-like tendencies. He liked to hang upside down from his tail. He was a much quieter, more affectionate animal than his elder brother. He had other eccentricities, too. In the wild, only the big apes walk on their knuckles; other monkeys tend to walk on the flat of their hands. But Nickit walked about with his fists clenched, putting gentle pressure on the knuckles of his hands. Maybe he picked up the habit from the 'Survival' programme on television.

Nickit used to ride about the park with me, hanging on to my neck or one of my arms. This was how he got invited to make his first major public appearance. One day we ran into a delightful party of schoolgirls on an outing to Kilverstone. I spent a long time with them chatting about the animals. A few months later, I received a letter from their head-mistress, saying that the girls had unanimously voted to have Lady Fisher to give out the prizes on their Speech Day. I was horrified, since I hate giving speeches and was never a great scholar. But I felt that I could hardly refuse. To ensure that no one fell asleep, I decided to take Nickit along.

A titter ran round the hall when we marched up to the platform. One thing to be said in favour of taking a baby monkey along on such occasions is that it is a certain way of distracting your audience from the hopeless mess that you are making of your own speech. I had brought Nickit in his gilded cage and put it down on the platform close to a table bearing a jug of water and a glass. The headmistress led off with a lengthy speech about the school's achievements. She had an unruly audience. A casual observer might have thought that Morecambe and Wise were on stage because everything that the headmistress said was greeted with guffaws. Nickit, realising at once that he had a captive audience, was making the most of the occasion. He was up to all his tricks – swinging on the bars, doing all sorts of acrobatics and thrusting his arm through the bars into the water jug. He would slurp the water up from his fingers. By the time I got up to deliver my speech, I doubt whether anyone was listening: Nickit was the centre of all eyes.

On another occasion, Brian had been spending time with Pinchit, who was adjusting to life in the monkey house after he had grown too old to stay on with us at Kilverstone Hall. Brian was rollicking around with Pinchit inside his cage and Pinchit was having a marvellous time, leaping back and forth from the branches to Brian's head or shoulders. They soon collected a sizeable crowd and, as I came strolling along with Tia and Nickit, I felt like shouting out, 'Roll up, roll up! Sixpence a look!'

Brian seemed to be delivering an impromptu lecture as different people in the audience, which had by now grown to about thirty, kept asking questions about Pinchit's habits, his family, what he was fed and so on. Suddenly, Brian's even tone changed abruptly.

'No, get out of it, you little horror,' he exploded.

A titter ran through the crowd.

'Hey, look out, chief,' an American in a loud check shirt yelled out, 'you're getting your head wet.'

And so he was. A rueful Brian was standing in the middle of the cage, with Pinchit squatting contemplatively on top of his tousled hair. Pee was running down Brian's face and into his beard.

A wag in the audience piped up, 'Is that good for your hair?'

It was too perfect an opportunity for the hirsute Brian to miss. 'You should try it, sir. The results are truly astonishing. Try a little of this every day and, as you can see, you'll be able to boast not only a full head of hair but a luxuriant beard to boot.'

Who knows? If the audience had shown any enthusiasm for the idea, we might have set up the Kilverstone Park Hair Tonic Company!

You will never see an Old World monkey hanging from a branch by its tail while it uses all four limbs to gather its food. This is just one of the many differences between Old World and New World monkeys. Another is that the monkeys of the New World are platyrrhines; that is to say, their nostrils are set wide apart with the openings to the sides. The teeming variety of New World species is exciting. The isolated jungle environments in which they have evolved have produced a dazzling array of colours and external characteristics. The New World is also remarkable for the only genuine night monkey in the world – the douroucouli.

We brought a family of douroucoulis, or 'owl monkeys', to Kilverstone. Their dense, soft fur makes them look larger than they really are. They have huge, saucer-shaped eyes with white patches above and below, and a widow's peak over their foreheads. The eyes, made to catch every trace of movement in the dark, dwarf their heads. If a human being had eyes of a comparable size in proportion to his head, they would be as big as grapefruit. The douroucoulis are shy, gentle creatures who spend most of the day sleeping in a hollow trunk or some other shady spot. At night in the wild they go hunting for small birds, insects, bats, fruit and leaves.

Apart from the marmosets and tamarins, who belong to a separate monkey family, the smallest creatures in the monkey houses at Kilverstone are the squirrel monkeys. Their appearance always makes me feel that they should be making television commercials for mustard. They have long, glove-like mustard fur along their hands and arms that make them look as if they have just been dipping into a gigantic mustard pot. Their backs are a pale olive green. They have tufted ears and white rings around eyes and ears, making the babies look exactly like pixies. They have long tails that they wrap round themselves like shawls when they go to sleep.

The squirrel monkeys – sometimes called 'half' monkeys –

are very quick and inquisitive, darting to and fro, determined to miss nothing. In the wild they spend most of their day trooping along beside a river, endlessly squabbling over choice morsels that are found along the way. In Peru I was told about the methods used by Indian trappers to snare them. The trappers put out bowls of sweetened water as a lure. When a large number of squirrel monkeys had gathered round a bowl the trappers would creep up and put some rum into the water. Before long this caused a high proportion of the monkeys to fall down, dead drunk.

It was a cruel trade. The squirrel monkeys were mostly caught for sale in the United States as pets but the trappers knew that baby squirrel monkeys would rarely survive the very harsh travelling conditions so they often abandoned babies that they had caught to die in the wild. Although many Latin American governments have now brought in very strict regulations to control the export of wildlife, including monkeys, the trade goes on. And apart from that, monkey stew is still a standard dish for many jungle-dwellers in areas where other kinds of meat are hard to come by.

We installed our two squirrel monkey families opposite each other in the monkey house. One consisted of a male and four females, called Little Jo, Little Mo, Little Bit and Little More. Just across the way from them was a couple called Pit and Pat, who would play out a full-scale Punch and Judy show every time they were given titbits, trying to jostle each other out of the way to hog the whole lot. The greatest delicacy for them was chicken. We would take down scraps and they would stuff their hands and mouths with it feverishly as if they had been fasting for a month. The marmosets and tamarins were equally keen on chicken. To our surprise the capuchins were not, although they were always ready to grab hold of any sparrow that happened to fall through their netting. Perhaps they preferred the taste of the raw meat. All the monkeys consumed vast quantities of insects with gusto; this is staple fare for the tree-dwelling monkeys of the New World.

The capuchins are by common consent the most intelligent of the New World monkeys. We imported both the white-fronted and the brown varieties, and we found that it did not take long for them to master quite a range of tricks. Looney, the dominant male among the brown capuchins, became very adroit with bolts and padlocks. On several occasions he managed to lock Stuart, the monkey keeper, into the next-door cage and he would have to shout until someone came to let him out while Looney looked on, delighted.

Looney left no one in his cage in any doubt about who was the boss. He looked a bit like a teddy-boy thug, with a quiff of dark hair over his forehead and dark patches at the sides that looked like sideboards. He certainly started out by living up to his teddy-boy image. He showed no apparent fear of any humans and would jump on to Stuart's back, pull his cap off and swing off towards the top of his cage, hooting with glee.

One day we brought in two young capuchins who had just come out of quarantine after their voyage from Peru. We called them Little Norman and Bashful. Little Norman could hardly have been more different in character from Looney. He was a shy, reflective little creature who liked to keep very much to himself.

Within a couple of weeks of Little Norman's arrival, Stuart was brought running to the cage by the most horrendous howls and shrieks. To his horror he found that Looney had just disposed of a baby capuchin that had been born to one of his females a few moments before. Looney had hauled the poor thing up to the roof of the cage, bitten it through the head and then dropped it. The body fell to the ground, where it lay in a tiny mangled heap. It had probably been killed by its father's bite.

We could not fathom out why Looney had attacked the

Jubilee, the baby jaguar, enjoys his bottle of milk.

Jason the Jaguar surveys the scene.

The beautiful eyes of this guanaco and her baby
would be the envy of any woman.

One of the Falabella foals born at Kilverstone
enjoys the spring sunshine.

Opposite above: Bandit, a baby racoon whom I hand-
reared, rides on his favourite toy.

Opposite below: A Capuchin monkey looking wistful.

John tickles Marcus and Malu, the lovely gentle tapirs.

Argentina and her first foal Red Rumba who loved to give great sloppy kisses.

Horrible Humphrey who became Royal Humphrey
after the Queen shook his tail.

baby but he was clearly not to be trusted with babies in future – or so we thought. To ensure that he would not get the chance to act in the same way again, we took Looney out of his cage just before another of the female brown capuchins gave birth. Stuart watched Looney closely over the following weeks and began to detect a kind of mellowing in his attitude to smaller monkeys. He seemed quite affectionate towards the new baby and was not tyrannising Little Norman quite so much.

When a female gave birth on Christmas Day to a baby male capuchin that we called Happy Christmas, or Happy for short, we decided to risk leaving Looney alone with the mother and baby. Looney turned out to be a reformed character. This time he proved to be a devoted father. When Happy grew big enough to leave his mother for short intervals, Looney would play with him and give him rides around the cage. Happy looked like a miniature Lester Piggott crouched on his back.

Little Norman was meanwhile displaying talents of a different kind. He proved to be a veritable Houdini. When he first came to Kilverstone, before moving him to the monkey house, we kept him for a time in the old stables where we had converted the loose boxes into big, airy cages. It was warm in there and so a good place to acclimatise animals that come straight from their quarantine quarters to the Norfolk cold.

In the stables we also bred grasshoppers to feed to the animals that were fond of insects, especially the marmosets and the squirrel monkeys. We kept the grasshoppers in a big glass box with sand at the bottom.

We should have thought more carefully. Capuchins are natural house-breakers. They are very clever at picking locks and unfastening catches and Little Norman was even more dexterous than Looney. One day he unfastened his own cage and let out Bashful, who was in there with him, at the same time. Once out he made straight for the glass box, worked out how to open the catch and settled in to a feast of grasshoppers.

Having finished his meal, he trotted off down the drive for a little post-prandial exercise. He walked for a mile or so until he got to the shepherd's cottage. The shepherd's wife, hearing Little Norman's 'pooh-pooh-pooh' sounds outside her kitchen window, thought that it must be a rabbit and nipped out to see whether she could pot it for her husband's supper. So we got Little Norman back, looking extremely pleased with himself.

He soon became a favourite with almost everyone, including even the bossy, temperamental Looney. Strangely enough, once Little Norman got on friendly terms with Looney, he found himself resented by some of the female brown capuchins, who seemed to be jealous of the favourable treatment he was getting. A mild war of the sexes developed inside the cage, which made us seriously worried at one stage that Bashful – the female at the absolute bottom of the pecking list – might not be getting enough to eat. After Looney and then Little Norman had had their fill of whatever food was put into the cage, the females would take it in turns, according to seniority, to hog what was left over. Bashful, being always at the end of the queue, seemed to be left with only a few scrapings. We eventually decided to resolve the problem by moving Bashful and Little Norman to a cage of their own.

Little Norman was delighted to have some new locks and equipment on which to flex his safecracker's wrists. One night he managed to crack Stuart's lock and escape into the outer room of his cage where he quickly found an alternative form of entertainment. He took on the rôle of electrician and did a thorough job of dismantling all the electrical plugs and sockets within his reach. He even took an electrical heater to bits. Fortunately they were all turned off. 'I wonder whether we should register him with the electricians' union,' John mused.

Next door to the brown capuchins we put a small family of woolly monkeys called Cecil, Cecily and Cecilia. Brazilian Indians sometimes refer to woolly monkeys as 'big bellies' because they tend to gorge themselves on fruit and nuts – and show it. Frank Muir is always delighted by Cecil, who has a mincing walk that he says reminds him of 'a pooftah actor'. Cecil certainly displayed little interest in females of his own species, although his response to females of the human sort convinces me that Frank was maligning him. The visits of Joyce, our dietician, for example, would throw Cecil into paroxysms of sexual excitement. Alas, he showed no such enthusiasm for Cecily or Cecilia.

Brian, the curator, was a stout defender of Cecil's reputation, insisting that eventually he would make good. He came in one evening to tell us that he had just spotted Cecil mounting one of the females but that, as soon as he realised he was being observed, he had got down with a sulky expression – 'just like a schoolboy caught doing something he shouldn't'.

'Really, Brian,' I exclaimed, 'that's quite unfair. How would you feel if someone had come and shone a torch into your bedroom? You really shouldn't go around like a Peeping Tom.'

But it wasn't just the Peeping Toms that put Cecil off. Eventually we were forced to conclude that he was just not the mating kind. We brought in another male, Max, who proved to be an energetic, if very aggressive, consort for Cecily and Cecilia. He would beat them up quite severely at the slightest provocation, and a beating from a male woolly monkey in his prime is not to be sneezed at. By the age of seven, when the male reaches sexual maturity, he is immensely strong.

The woolly monkeys are the only monkeys at Kilverstone whose cage I would not go into alone. They have their dedicated admirers in Britain – indeed, a whole colony of woolly monkeys has been established in the west country – but even the most experienced breeders have suffered some savage bites and bruises. The woolly monkey has a formidable set of jaws. In one British zoo we know, they had been keeping their woolly monkeys in a fairly low cage. One day, one of the male woolly monkeys was hanging by his tail from the roof of the cage and took the girl keeper by surprise as she came in the door. Such was the strength of the monkey's massive biceps that he was able to lift the poor girl off the ground and ripped her arm open before she could escape. She needed fifteen stitches.

I doubt whether it is possible to establish a complete rapport with a woolly monkey, although we know a number of people who have tried. One man whom we know reared a male woolly monkey from its infancy. He had it with him for much of the time: it ate with him, slept with him and travelled with him all over the place. They became virtually inseparable. Despite this, the woolly monkey flew into a temper one day and bit him very deeply on the thigh.

After the first three years among the monkeys I developed a real appreciation for the varieties of emotion that monkeys can express through their speech, their gestures and their facial movement. It is of course nonsense to make out that monkeys do not have the gift of speech. Efforts have been made to classify the dazzling vocabulary of sounds and intonations that the marmoset and the capuchin employ in their daily lives.

The spider monkeys are perhaps my favourites in the monkey houses because they are the most demonstratively affectionate. Eric, the black spider monkey from Peru, would shake hands with everyone who passed as if he were standing at the head of a diplomatic reception line. He was always terribly enthusiastic when he saw me or Trina. He would greet us from a distance and then when one of us got up alongside the cage he would stretch his long arms through the cage in a tight embrace, making slurpy kissing noises on the cheek. It could be a bit uncomfortable, and if he got me round the neck I felt rather as if I was being throttled; there was surprising strength in those wiry black arms. But if Eric did not get his cuddle and I just walked by, affecting to ignore him, he would let out hysterical screams. There's not much difference between human babies and my jungle babies.

8

The Plague of Giant Rats

It is sad but true that the biggest boost a safari park can have is if some unfortunate gets mauled by one of the big cats. This seems to arouse the public's excitement. After one such incident had happened at another park, I said to John, 'Do you think we should feed one of the children to Jason the jaguar?'

We had a different sort of windfall at the end of our third year. There was a nine-day wonder in the local press about a new parrot disease that was going the rounds and a local MP suggested that it might have come from the East Anglian wildlife parks. It was a totally unfounded allegation, as was quickly proved when an investigation was carried out. But the scare focused more people's attention on the existence of Kilverstone, and the publicity, even though hostile, did us good. And we needed it – when the figures were added up, we found that far from reaching the 100,000 which was our target for that year, we had done little better than stand still. Only 70,000 had visited the park and our accountant's face was growing longer and longer. I was particularly disappointed as I had just heard that there was a chance of buying a maned wolf from behind the Iron Curtain. Since our trip to Panama I had set my heart on acquiring an example of this rare and endangered species and on eventually establishing a family from which we could breed. But even I found it hard to argue with the dismal figures.

More excitement was caused by what the local press called the 'plague of giant rats'. I remember vividly the morning the scare began. It was still dark when the telephone rang. John blearily hauled himself out of bed to answer it. Nickit, the capuchin monkey, snuggled down in the crook of my arm, peeped out over the edge of the blanket, let out an ill-tempered squeak and cuddled back into the warmth.

John usually talks in a whisper, and at this time of day he was even more subdued than normal. So it was hard to make out what was going on until he suddenly bellowed into the receiver, 'Giant rats? What the hell are you talking about?'

There were explanatory squawks from the other end.

Combing his fingers through his hair, John said, 'Look, the animals which have escaped are not rats. They are called capybaras. Cap-y-bar-as. They are harmless, peace-loving creatures. No, they are not going to kill anyone, they're not even going to bite anyone.'

More squawks.

'No, they don't carry the plague, or any other disease. Haven't you heard of quarantine? What's that? You want to come over to Kilverstone? What radio programme did you say you were on? Well, if you bloody well want to come, come at a civilised hour. And don't come expecting to see some monster out of "Dr Who".'

John slammed down the receiver and treated Nickit and me, in a few choice phrases, to his views on journalists who telephone at five in the morning.

The night before the reporter rang, we had had the kind of storm that makes you wish you had a concrete shelter. The lightning forked across the sky and the wind tore down hundreds of trees on the estate. Bruce the capybara, his wife Sheila (we had given her this dinkum-Aussie name because 'Bruce' sounds so Australian), and some of their family headed off for the river. We had spent all night looking for them and had only been in bed for an hour or two when the reporter rang.

'Can you imagine?' said John. 'That so-and-so actually asked me whether Bruce would spring at people's throats and rip them apart. They seem to think he'll swim down the river to Thetford and pop up outside the supermarket to massacre the shoppers. The idiot even asked me whether the police shouldn't put out an announcement advising farmers to shoot him on sight.'

'Poor Bruce,' I sighed. 'They just don't understand you.'

Unhappily for Bruce, the word 'rodent' makes people think of rats. The capybara is a rodent – in fact, the world's largest rodent – but you would have a better idea of its appearance and temperament if you thought of it as the world's largest guinea-pig. The word 'rodent', which makes people think of dirty things that bite, has a very inoffensive origin. It is derived from the Latin verb 'to gnaw' and it applies to the hundreds of different species like mice, guinea-pigs and capybaras which are fortunate enough to have split-level teeth. Like other rodents, the capybara can tuck its upper and lower incisors inside each other like scissor blades. While it is gnawing away at something with its front teeth it can close off the back of its mouth so that splinters and unsavoury fragments don't get through. It can then fold its front teeth together, fitting the lower incisors inside the upper ones, while it laboriously chews up its meal with its sturdy back teeth.

Apart from the useful arrangement of its teeth, the capybara has nothing in common with the rat. It is a shy, family-conscious, ruminative creature that lives almost entirely on grass or vegetation. It spends most of its day placidly grazing or diving to the bottom of a river bed to pull up the plants that grow there. Although capybaras have been known to eat fish they are essentially herbivorous. They do not prey upon man; man preys upon them. Their flesh is served up as a particular delicacy in wayside food-stalls in the Andes countries, often garnished with a piquant red-pepper sauce.

The capybara shunts clumsily and jerkily about on land, which is not surprising, since it has to support up to 150 lb. on its little stubby legs. It comes into its own in the water, where it swims about like a hippo with just the eyes and the snout breaking the surface. If it is paddling along in a shallow stream it will propel itself by kicking its feet against the river bed. In deeper waters it swims with its hind legs, spreading its webbed feet on the downstroke like a duck.

Capybaras will spend a third of their day lazing and swimming about in the water. Their favourite time to bathe is the early evening. The water is also the place where capybaras like to be in the mating season. The courtship of a pair of capybaras in a river bend is a joy to watch. They swim and slither around each other in intricate patterns, diving again and again. They celebrate the occasion with a high-pitched bird-like call, a cross between a cheep and a whistle.

Bruce was our first capybara and the long record of his escapes is almost an animal Colditz saga. The pursuit of Bruce and his relatives became such a regular pastime for the keepers that they talked of it as 'cappy-hunting'.

I don't think that Bruce broke out because he regarded Kilverstone as a concentration camp; at least, I hope not. The capybara is a timid creature. When it is frightened, its hair stands on end and its first instinct, wherever it happens to be, is to head for water. In the wild, capybaras will dive into a river to escape a jaguar. At Kilverstone, a thunderstorm or a night intruder would send Bruce careering through the fences into the river Thet, often followed by his wife and offspring. Like all capybaras he is superbly built to shoulder his way through the thickest undergrowth and there are few fences that will hold him if he had made up his mind to get through.

Come the morning, we all set off down the river again to look for the capybaras. Brian Dickson and his wife, Jean, piled into a rowing boat to do some reconnaissance. Jean is a strapping, commonsensical girl but she has always been frightened of water and has never learned to swim. We rushed her into the boat before she had time to think about it. She jumped into the stern and Brian, who was standing in the bow, was catapulted up into the air. Jean laughed so much that she quite forgot her fear.

But neither Brian nor Jean proved to be much of an oarsman. They set off, both sitting in the stern of the boat, so that every time Brian pulled on the oars the boat jerked and swayed with its bow sticking up in the air. We called to them to spread their weight and Brian moved up into the bow. Everything went smoothly until they found themselves heading straight for a tree. Jean grabbed for a branch, missed and went toppling into the river. Brian managed to grab hold of her and pull her out.

'Good training for the cappies,' called out one of the keepers. 'Reckon you can do that with Bruce?'

Rowing back upstream, Brian found two of the younger capybaras wallowing about in the muddy bank of the bream pool. They shot back into the scrub. Brian decided that the most likely way to bag them was to lay a net since, as soon as they are startled, they will charge straight towards the nearest water. With the help of two keepers, Keith and Peter, Brian rigged up a net and staked it along the river-bank. We all went hallooing through the bushes, trying to make the capybaras break cover and rush into the net. After much shouting and thrashing about in the scrub, the first animal to break cover was Bruce himself. To our dismay, he started to gallop ponderously in exactly the wrong direction, heading straight towards Keith. Brian was jumping up and down and shouting instructions, but in his excitement he tripped and went sprawling into the net, where he managed to get himself completely tangled up. As he lay there panting, we heard a howl and two splashes. Bruce had charged straight past Keith, sending him reeling back over the bank and into the river, and then flopped down into the water himself and set off at a brisk dog-paddle in the direction of Thetford.

'Hey look! We've got one!' shouted Peter.

Everyone was laughing so much at the sight of Brian struggling in the net, puffing his lips like a fish, that we lost the chance to head off the retreat of the other members of Bruce's family.

While Keith and Brian were shaking themselves down, I went back to the house to feed Nickit and to get lunch together for the guests we were expecting that day. The phone rang in the kitchen. It was our early-morning caller again.

'Oh yes, you're the man who wants to know about the giant rats,' I said. 'I'm afraid we haven't caught them yet.'

He wanted to come and see the chase but I felt that I couldn't really invite him down to see the Charlie Chaplin show that John and the keepers were enacting by the river. So I promised that we would give him an interview later that day.

'You know, you've started quite a panic,' he said. 'People are ringing in to say that they've seen your animals all over the place.' A man who was picked up for drunken driving had told the police that he had been unable to stick to one side of the road because of 'this great black thing that kept zigzagging in front of me'. Someone else swore that one of the capybaras had been chasing his chickens. I can see why eye-witness accounts of accidents or robberies are often so unreliable.

I was mixing up the milk for Nickit's bottle when the phone rang again.

'Is that Lady Fisher?' asked a man's voice.

'Who is speaking, please?'

'You don't know me, Lady Fisher, I'm calling from Leicester. I just wanted to say that I've seen one of your cap . . . cappies . . . the big rats.'

'In *Leicester*?' Unless it had sprouted wings, there was no way that one of our capybaras could have got from Kilverstone to Leicester in a few hours. 'What did it look like?'

'It was darkish-like with a big, bushy tail and it was shinning up a tree. I didn't go too close, you know.'

'Thank you very much. I'm afraid that capybaras don't have tails and they don't climb trees. And they do *not* bite.'

We have been getting similar phone calls ever since.

John came back, muddy and crestfallen, at about half past one. Over the roast lamb our guests offered their advice on how to retrieve Bruce and his family. There was much talk of lassoes and traps and dart guns. Probably the most sensible suggestion was that we should try to keep Bruce underwater until he was tired out and gave up the game. But capybaras can stay submerged for up to eight or ten minutes, and swim a fair distance in that time, and I suspected that we would be tired out first.

We decided that we would have to try to catch the capybaras in the water, where they have only one means of escape – to dive underwater. So the keepers chased Bruce up and down the river in the rowing boat all afternoon while John and I tramped back and forth along the bank with the net, waiting to bag him. Bruce seemed to be getting the better of us. Every time the boat was swung to within paddle distance he would hiss and grunt and dive underwater in a great wallowing motion. Then his snout would pop up again on the other side of the boat, out of reach.

Bruce could swim rings round all of us and our main worry was that he might head all the way downstream to return to dry land where the river Thet flows through the shopping precinct in Thetford – where the advance publicity he had been receiving would no doubt inspire a general panic. Every time he seemed to be swimming too far away in that direction, the keepers would paddle madly to overtake him and head him off.

As dusk fell and the Norfolk chill began to seep into our bones we still had not managed to lure Bruce out of the water. Peter, the head keeper, decided on desperate measures. In the failing light he plunged his arms into the water and managed to get a grip on Bruce's hind legs.

It was a risky operation for Bruce was not much smaller than the rowing boat, and as he bucked and slithered about it tipped and turned at alarming angles. While Keith leaned over the other side of the boat, trying to balance the weight, Stuart, the monkey keeper, caught hold of Peter's waist in an effort to stop him from being jerked overboard.

The keepers were soaked through when they finally managed to heave Bruce into the boat, and there was so much water sloshing about inside the hull that it looked as if it might sink before they got their prize to shore. But they made it. John put his arms round Bruce's middle, and with Peter holding on to his hind legs the capybara only needed an apple in his mouth to resemble a roast pig. But Bruce still had some fight left in him. Back on land he started hissing and trying to bite. At long last he was shoved into an open-work sack. We rigged up a sort of stretcher for him on which he was laid and lugged back to his enclosure. By now the sky was pitch-dark, and the wind was biting.

'Right,' said John, 'I think we'll call it quits for today. At least we can say to the press that we caught the ringleader of the giant rats.'

'I expect the others will trot along before the night's out,' said Brian. 'They won't have gone far down the river and I bet they won't want to stay out in the cold on a night like this. I'll put out some more food for them and sit up to give them a welcome if they come.'

Sure enough, Sheila came home before dawn with most of her children in tow. We were able to take the local press down to show them what Bruce looked like.

The man who had been terrorising the public with tales of giant rats got short shrift. 'They do look quite peaceable,' he grudgingly admitted. 'You haven't had a jaguar escape by any chance, have you?'

This was by no means the end of Bruce's career as an escapologist, although we could hardly blame him for running off on the following New Year's Eve when an intruder – no doubt the worse for drink – went stumbling into his paddock. Bruce was cosily tucked up with his family in their three-bedroomed house. He was so frightened that, remarkably for a capybara, he did a high jump through the window. The sad thing was that in his panic he forgot the rule about women and children first: he trampled two of Sheila's latest litter and when we found them in the morning, both were dead.

Fortunately Bruce and Sheila were an enthusiastic husband and wife and in four years at Kilverstone they had twenty-eight babies, most of whom survived. Capybaras can produce offspring from the age of eight months and the period of gestation is about 120 days. Sheila's litters varied in number from three to five. As some of the male capybaras grew older, however, there was trouble in the pen as Bruce set out to make it plain exactly who was the boss.

Timid and inoffensive creatures though they may be, capybaras – both male and female – insist on a very strict social pecking-order. An ambitious young male who takes too much interest in the dominant male's favourite female or challenges his authority in other ways runs the risk of having to defend himself against savage bites or being driven out of the herd completely.

The latter seems to have been the fate of one of Bruce's male children who was beginning to take an active interest in sex. In keeping with the incongruously Australian flavour of Bruce's and Sheila's names, we had called this one Barry MacKenzie after the spoof films about the adventures of a beer-swilling Australian innocent abroad. Barry started to annoy his father and the keepers noticed a few scuffles in their enclosure. Then Barry was off into the wild blue yonder. I think that the message from Bruce must have been, 'Go west, young man. Go and fend for yourself and find a wife somewhere else.'

Barry did not content himself with a leisurely paddle down the river as in previous escapes. He was last reported in the direction of Bury St Edmunds, probably seeking a young capybara bride among the cornfields and pheasant-shoots. It was a hopeless expedition and it ended tragically. Waddling across a road, Barry was run over by a car. The driver said afterwards that she thought she had killed a bear.

This is probably the only occasion when one of our capybaras has tried to push off for other parts. There has been a pattern to all the other escapes: Bruce and his family were trying to get to running water. Most often they would simply be taking advantage of someone's negligence in leaving a gate open in order to have a relaxing paddle in the river Thet. When frightened they would behave the same way as their cousins in the wild when confronted by a jaguar, a puma or a man with a gun – heading for water and relying on their ability to outswim their natural predators.

The comforting thing for us was to find that Bruce and Sheila know where home is. During a thunderstorm, John was wandering about in his anorak, counting the trees that had been bowled over, when he came face to face with Bruce, who was quietly sitting outside the door of his house. He had bolted again from the thunder and now he wanted to get back into the warmth. He knew where he belonged.

We have breakfast at Kilverstone in a big, airy room with steps leading down to the orangery. For a new arrival it is startling to look out over the toast-rack, through the tall windows, and see bison grazing in stately fashion on the back lawn. People of nervous disposition invariably ask us whether the bison are likely to charge the house. In fact we have our secret defences. Between the lawn and the field where the bison graze is a ha-ha, a hidden ditch, that was the focus for some hair-raising thrills and spills when the boys took to racing a go-kart.

I suppose it is a bit of a cheek to keep bison in a Latin American zoo since these great horned and bearded creatures are basically natives of the North American plains. But the bison herds, in their heyday before the white man got to work on them, did range freely through Mexico and the Southern states of the USA so we thought we had sufficient excuse. We started with a pair that we called William and Mary.

William was a grand old man, weighing a good 1,800 lb., who watched the world go by with a choleric eye. He turned out to be a surprisingly good father. When their first baby was born he licked it all over and started clearing up the mess. We watched this display of paternal concern from a cautious distance, lying spreadeagled on the pathway between the deer park and the bisons' enclosure and peering through a pair of binoculars. In the North American prairies in the old days bison were frequently wiped out by hunters because of their close family feelings. If a cow was giving birth the rest of the herd would circle round the mother and the new-born until the baby was strong enough to get up on its feet and follow the herd. Hunters would come across a bison herd protecting its young in this way and wipe them all out.

Geoffrey, the keeper who was in charge of the bison baby, wanted to call it Bertie.

'But Geoffrey,' I protested, 'you can't possibly call it Bertie. That's a boy's name, and this is a girl.'

'But milady,' he said, 'there are lots of girls called Bertie.

I used to go to the cinema every Saturday night with a girl called Bertie.' He looked so forlorn that I decided Bertie it must be.

Geoffrey had supervised every detail of Bertie's birth and had been horrified to see the baby simply allowed to drop to the ground by its mother. 'What's she doing to my baby?' he shouted. We only realised later that, just as human babies are smacked on the bottom to get them breathing properly, baby bison are allowed to fall to the ground in order to shake them up. A new-born bison is not dark like its parents but has a chestnut colour, rather like a Guernsey calf, which it closely resembles at this stage. Later it develops dark patches and begins to look a bit moth-eaten as it gradually turns into a replica of its parents.

Bison, although huge, are fairly pacific-looking creatures and few people seem to realise that they can threaten anyone or anything in their way if they have a mind to do so.

The summer after Bertie was born, Geoffrey had gone down to the bisons' field and found an easel with a half-finished picture of the house roughed out in water-colours. He was terribly frightened that the artist had been trampled down by William. He looked around the pen to see whether anyone was there and then ran down to the riverside walk to see if the artist had gone off for a stroll. He came back, increasingly worried. He was standing scratching his head by the bison pen when he saw a girl walking down the back lawn across the park, apparently about to leap over the ha-ha back into the bison field. He blew the whistle which he always wears around his neck to keep the visitors in order and gestured frantically at her to stop. He rushed over and shouted, 'Please don't come any further, it's terribly dangerous.'

'Nonsense,' she said firmly, 'I've been sitting in the bison field for an hour or more. I was perfectly comfortable with my back to the tree and the bison sniffing around. They're not going to hurt anybody.'

Perhaps William and Mary appreciated her artistry. But it really is safer not to take any chances with 1,800 lb. of bison. Their tempers are notoriously short-fused.

When we had had Bertie for almost two years and the herd had grown to half a dozen, a strange and very frightening episode took place that we still find hard to understand. It was an eruption of violence of a kind that we have rarely experienced at Kilverstone. Bertie had reached sexual maturity and was in season. Animals do not observe the same sexual inhibitions as humans and she had spent a morning scampering about and making up to her father, behaving in a quite provocative way. He was apparently angered by these advances because he butted her a few times to send her off. Clearly he did not think this was the right way for his daughter to behave towards him. He butted her so hard with his huge, hairy head that he knocked her to the ground.

We heard about what ensued from a family who had been watching from the other side of the fence. They said that the other bison had gathered round and looked as if they were trying to hoist her up by her horns back on to her feet. But after a while they flew into a collective frenzy. William and Mary and the other bison took turns to kneel on Bertie's back, dealing her terrible blows with their horns.

'Help, help!' one of the visitors yelled. John, the butler, was just down the path with the penguins and came running. But by the time he got there, Bertie had been horned to death. Forlornly, we got the vet round to do an autopsy.

He confirmed that Bertie had been at the peak of her season. 'I don't quite understand it,' he said, 'but this must have been the stimulating factor. Maybe bison have taboos, like humans.'

For many days afterwards, the other bison seemed to be terribly upset that Bertie was dead. William fell into an obvious sulk, mooching around and rejecting all human advances.

9

Rudolf and Mrs Wolf

'We'll have to sell another picture.'

All through that winter at the end of our disappointing third year, I had been haunted by the thought of the maned wolves and of the contribution which I felt we at Kilverstone should make to their survival. Now I had hit upon the only way we could afford to buy one. Even the accountant had to give his grudging agreement, and so Rudolf arrived at Kilverstone from Prague Zoo.

A native of northern Argentina, Paraguay and the far south of Brazil, the maned wolf has steadily retreated before man's advance, fleeing the farmer's gun and the encroaching cotton plantations to take refuge in the marshes of the Gran Chaco in Paraguay. It has become so rare that it rates a stud-book in which all the maned wolves that have been reported to be living in captivity are described and numbered. Rudolf is number twenty-four.

The maned wolf is a timid creature. It is not dangerous to man and is not a pest to farmers, unlike the fox, since it is never known to attack livestock or hens. I have met Argentinian ranchers who shoot the maned wolf on sight, claiming that it attacks their lambs but I don't believe that this actually happens. For one thing the maned wolf is hardly carnivorous at all. In the wild it will pick up small bits of carrion and hunt little birds and rodents, insects and reptiles. But the main part of its diet consists of fruit and vegetables. It loves wild figs and the fruit of the *Solanum gladiflora* tree, which is known as a result as 'the fruit of the wolf'.

Knowing that maned wolves are shy, nervous animals, we wanted to avoid frightening Rudolf when he first arrived at Kilverstone so we decided to put him as far away as possible from the main flow of visitors. We built him a special pen tucked away behind the alpacas' paddocks and stables.

Rudolf looked rather like a fox on stilts, with bits and pieces borrowed from other animals which fit together in a kind of quivering beauty. He was a rusty reddish colour with a ridge of blackish hair down his back which bristled when he got excited. He had huge, bat-like ears lined with white hair, which waved about like radar screens when some smaller animal like a vole or a mouse crossed his pen.

Getting to know Rudolf required a great deal of patience. I would go down each day and talk to him from the other side of the wire, tossing small pieces of fruit into his pen and giving him time to get used to my presence and the sound of my voice. I found that he was particularly fond of bananas, dried figs and dates. As we got to know each other better, I would offer him some of these delicacies with my fingers. The next step was to go inside the pen and coax him to come up to me to feed from my hand. He gathered confidence and would soon come running up when he saw me coming. But if other people came, particularly in a group clicking cameras, he would still shy away and go bounding off to the farthest corner of his pen.

Rudolf had an extraordinary eating habit; the only other animal in which I have observed it is Tia, my chihuahua. Despite the dramatic difference in their appearance there must be a family relationship between these two New World dogs. Sometimes, when given a piece of fruit, Rudolf would bend down until he was pressing it with his shoulder. He would then swivel back and forth, crushing it to a pulp, before finally eating it. Tia also liked to play with titbits of food in this way – but there is a considerable difference between a tiny chihuahua rolling about with a bit of fruit and someone trying to perform the same act on stilts.

A year after Rudolf came to Kilverstone we were delighted to find a mate for him, a female from the wild whom we called simply Mrs Wolf. Rudolf bullied her mercilessly. I could only ever manage to give her titbits by stealth. If he saw me trying to slip her food, Rudolf would run up and shoo her off in order to hog it for himself.

At about the same time another British zoo imported a pair of maned wolves, the only others that we knew about in the country. Tragically, their keeper (as I later heard) insisted on treating them like ordinary wolves and fed them on a solid diet of meat. 'Whoever heard of a wolf that lived on fruit,' he snorted when one of our keepers tried to put him right. Within a couple of months both the maned wolves fell ill, and they died within days of each other.

We were given a third maned wolf, whom we called Bramble, by London Zoo. It was encouraging to know that they thought we were the experts on rearing maned wolves in captivity. It is certainly a worthwhile task, since the maned wolf is today in real danger of extinction in its native habitat.

The maned wolves of Kilverstone also became the subject for a delicate, important line of medical research. A medical specialist from the University of Pennsylvania telephoned one day to ask if he could visit us to collect urine specimens from the maned wolves. It seems that they have a very small urethra, like man, and the American expert hoped that by studying the maned wolves it might be possible to learn something about the causes of stones in the urethra to which man is liable because of his physical make-up.

We spent a fairly grisly morning laying out plastic sheets and encouraging Rudolf, Mrs Wolf and Bramble to drink as much as they could. Bramble performed splendidly, producing a thimbleful. Rudolf sprayed the wall and produced only a small wet patch on a piece of blotting paper. (Such are the wonders of modern science that we were told this was all that was required.) Mrs Wolf produced nothing at all. I am told that maned wolves have the extraordinary capacity of being able to absorb and concentrate their urine so that they can survive for an entire week without passing water.

As time passed, the maned wolves became more and more confident about being in the presence of humans, responding to my coaxing during my daily visits. We decided to build them two large runs and to put up two semi-detached houses for them to live in. There was one pen for Rudolf and Mrs Wolf, another for Bramble. We had decided that until we could find Bramble a mate we weren't going to allow any wife-swapping between the maned wolves – although in some ways I would not have blamed Mrs Wolf if she had decided to swap partners. Rudolf was very much the male chauvinist, hogging the best food for himself. Instead of being attracted to the more gentlemanly Bramble, however, Mrs Wolf took a savage bite at his paw when he pushed it through the wire of their pen one day, probably only wanting to shake hands.

The urine-collecting American professor had been studying maned wolves all over the world. I was thrilled when he told us that he had never seen any as tame and unconcerned in the presence of humans as Rudolf and his family and that ours were the only ones he could get near.

'Go for the neck!' shouted John. 'That's right. Get it by the throat!'

Brian Dickson, purple-faced and sweating profusely, got his fist around the neck of Stumper, our male rhea. The rhea is a big, terrestrial bird, a smaller cousin of the ostrich, that makes up for its inability to fly by sprinting along the ground on its long, bony legs. The only way I know to deal with an angry rhea is to seize it by the neck and hold it at arm's length. But you need very long arms to do this safely.

It was the mating season and Stumper had become unusually testy. We had had to catch him because he had just been venting his spleen on some boys who were fishing down by the river. Perhaps he thought they were rivals.

'Ouch!' Brian complained. Without thinking, he had bent his elbow far enough to enable Stumper to deliver a powerful kick. Brian quickly thrust his arm back so that Stumper hung suspended just above the ground, his legs swishing back and forth like hockey sticks.

The danger is that rheas, like many wild birds, are easily panicked and can die without warning if they are too frightened. We had been warned that you should never chase a rhea for more than twenty minutes or so, or its heart might stop dead. We carefully wrapped Stumper up in a duffle coat. We put his legs through the arms of the coat and his head and body in the rest with the curator's hat over his eyes and beak: any bird or animal is calmer in the dark. But alas, Stumper died as we carried him back to his enclosure. Brian massaged his heart and tried to bring him back to life but without success.

We had Stumper's wife, Pecker, and two younger rheas left. One of them, Stella, was a white, freckly and empty-headed female. We moved them to a new enclosure after Stumper died, next to the large, caged-in area where we kept Rudolf and Mrs Wolf. We would have warned the rheas, if we could have done, that although the maned wolf's diet consists largely of fruit, they enjoy gobbling up birds and small rodents and had already chalked up a great tally of John's pheasants before the rheas moved in as their neighbours.

But we could not have expected that Stella, out of idle curiosity, would stroll up to the cage and stick her head through the wire. The moment she poked her beak through, one of the maned wolves leaped into the air. Before she had time to retreat, the wolf sank its teeth into her neck.

Luckily for Stella, the jaws of a maned wolf are not quite as strong as those of its European cousin and instead of chopping her head off, the wolf stripped off nine inches of skin exactly as if it were peeling a banana. When Stella managed to pull her neck and head away, the loose skin was left dangling from the top of her head with a completely raw, bloody neck below. We found her in a shivering heap and almost gave up hope of saving her on the spot. It was not just that she looked gruesome; after our experience with Stumper, we were sure that the shock alone would kill her. We rushed to the telephone to call Bill Marriott, the local vet. He was out on a call but picked up our message on his radio telephone and dashed over at once.

'It doesn't look good,' Mr Marriott said. 'We'll just have to hope that her heart will hold out. What we need is a good cobbler to stitch her back together again,' Mr Marriott called one of his colleagues, who drove over and helped him stitch the skin back on to Stella's neck.

'It's pretty rough surgery, I'm afraid,' said the vet. 'I can't swear that this is going to work. The skin may well dry out and die like parchment.'

As Stella lay there trembling, with a criss-cross of stitching all up her neck, turning a bloodshot, disconsolate eye towards us, I felt very sombre about her chances of pulling through.

To our surprise and relief she was able to walk again and beginning to regain her appetite within a few days. But something very strange had happened to her neck. Rheas have very supple necks that they can twist a long way in either direction but Stella's neck looked as though someone had wrenched it round by force so that the beak pointed straight back over her tail. If we stood behind her she was facing us. If we stood in front of her we saw the back of her head. We sent for Mr Marriott again.

'Don't you think if we just grabbed her head and twisted it round that might do the trick?' I asked him.

He looked glum. 'Oh dear,' he said, 'I'm afraid I couldn't take responsibility for that. I'll probably need to put Stella under a general anaesthetic and take a closer look at her.'

But for no apparent reason Stella had picked up remarkably by the following day. Her head was still akilter but her beak was firmly pointed to the left instead of straight behind, which seemed to us a great improvement. She was also eating more although we still had to feed her by hand. There was a great, ugly, mulberry-coloured scab all the way down her neck but it did not seem to be pulling and hurting her as much as before. Mr Marriott advised us to let nature take its own course. In the days that followed Stella's head swung little by little back into its normal position. Within five weeks the scab had fallen away and she looked as perky and flippant as usual. Nature had done more than we could in a situation which had looked almost beyond healing.

10

Camels of the Incas

Chocolate Drop, the black alpaca, and Juan the guanaco were two of the veterans of Kilverstone. They were with us from the earliest days of the wildlife park, and they had to put up with a great deal. For a start they were both males and we had trouble at the outset in finding mates for them. In those early days Juan would amuse himself by biting great lumps of fur out of Chocolate Drop, who had a docile nature. Luckily for Chocolate Drop we at last found for Juan a bride whom we called Juanita. Otherwise there would have been a fair chance that Juan would have plucked the alpaca bald.

Juan and Juanita settled down to producing a boy guanaco every year, starting with their very first season. But their family life was not exactly calm. Juan became increasingly jealous of his sons and one year he flew at the eldest and tore off his ear. Bill Marriott, the vet, did a wonderful job of patching him up and we learned our lesson: we started a new herd. We brought a pale blonde bride for Juan's eldest son – henceforth known as One Ear – from Whipsnade Zoo, and they set up house in a paddock of their own.

After much scouring about we came up with a suitable bride for Chocolate Drop as well, a brown alpaca with protruding buck teeth whom we called Bovril, and another male and female whom we called Andes and Chili-Bean. They produced a splendid all-white foal christened Polo Mint.

One sweltering summer when the alpaca herd had grown to five, we decided that we must shear the alpacas. The difficulty was to find a man to do the job. We found that our tenant farmer's son had just come back from Australia, where he had spent some time with the sheep shearers, one of the hardiest breeds of farm workers in the world. We persuaded him to take on the job with the aid of a couple of our keepers to hold the alpacas down. Chocolate Drop was the first to be shorn and he clearly thought that we were playing the same trick on him that Delilah played on Samson. After he had lost his luxuriant curls he was extremely shame-faced and cantered off to hide himself from public view. The others reacted the same way.

The effects of this 'Samson complex' were quite extra-ordinary. Brian, the curator, had suggested that we should only shear the adult alpacas and not bother about a nine-month-old foal that Chocolate Drop had sired. But the young male became aggressively frisky when his seniors had had their hair chopped off, obviously feeling that he was the only one who had kept his virility. He even made im-proper advances to his mother.

'Off with his hair,' John instructed. 'That's the only thing for it.'

Our collection of 'Andean sheep' would not have been complete without the most familiar members of the family, the llamas. They were also the possessors of exaggerated Bugs Bunny teeth and liable to spit at people they didn't like if their patience was tested too far. The llama and its cousins were central to the lives of the Incas in ancient Peru, in fact they were pillars of the Inca economy.

The Spanish chronicler, Agustin de Zarate, who travelled to Peru in the footsteps of the conqueror Pizarro, first des-cribed the llamas and alpacas as 'Peruvian sheep'. But he also noticed their resemblance to their cousins, the camels of Africa and the Middle East. 'One of the characteristics of these Peruvian sheep', Zarate wrote, 'is that they can carry a load of fifty or sixty pounds like camels, which they much resemble in build though they have no hump. Spaniards have since used them as horses, for they can carry a man four or five leagues in a day. When they are tired and lie on the ground, they will not get up even if beaten or pulled; the only thing to do is to take off their load. If they grow tired when ridden and the rider urges them on, they will turn their heads and spatter him with a very evil-smelling liquid which they seem to carry in their crops.'

The llamas' wild relations, the guanacos and vicuñas, roamed the hunting grounds, which all belonged to the Inca emperor. No one was allowed to hunt in them without his permission or that of his governor. In particular, the people of one province were not allowed to hunt or interfere with animals in another province. The emperor, like the authorities in modern times, granted a hunting licence only for certain seasons or for limited quantities of meat or wool when there was a national shortage. It was always forbidden to kill females. Vicuñas were captured alive for their wool which was greatly valued by the Inca élite. Slings and nooses were used to capture them once they had been driven into the centre of a circle of hunters.

An American came to stay with us, a friend of John's sister who lives in Philadelphia. When we took him down to the paddocks where Chocolate Drop, Juan and the llamas were grazing, he asked us, 'Do you eat your llamas often?'

'No!' we exclaimed simultaneously, absolutely horrified.

The American explained that he had a rancher friend in New Mexico who kept llamas as well as cattle and would barbecue one of them for a lunch party whenever he felt that the herd was getting overstocked. The meat, he cautioned us, is pretty tough.

He also warned us that it was dangerous to try to hand-rear a llama. Accustomed to getting food from the human hand, it can then fly into a paroxysm of rage if its keeper or owner turns up without the expected titbits. A llama's line of attack can be terrifying. Llamas have been known to rear up behind a keeper and bring their hooves crashing down on to his skull.

At the end of our fourth year at the zoo, John and I revisited Peru, the home of the 'camels of the Incas'. We flew from a horrid slushy January in London into brilliant sunshine, which was a much-needed tonic. Just before we left we had heard that the elusive 100,000 had once again slipped through our fingers – our attendance for the year had risen to no more than 85,000. But by now there was no going back; the animals were part of our family and it was unthinkable to abandon them, although I had had to put material on the wall to cover the gaps left by the pictures we had been forced to sell to make ends meet.

Waiting at Lima airport to greet us were our friends Felipe and Marie Louise Benavides with their white Land-Rover with its big World Wildlife Fund badge.

We drove straight out to their home, a pale, pink-washed house surrounded by a pale, pink-washed wall, entered by one of three colonial Spanish wooden gates. The one on the left led to the garage, the one on the right was the one we had gone through on previous visits. The centre gate, according to the family, had only ever been opened three times – once for Lady Mountbatten, once for Prince Bertil of Sweden and once for the marriage of Felipe's daughter.

'So what gate did Prince Philip use when he came out to see you?' I asked Felipe as he held the door open for me.

'Why, the same gate the Fishers use, of course,' he cheerily replied.

It was in fact the most charming gateway of all, the archway covered in a large flowering jasmine which sends out a wonderful, all-pervasive smell. The first thing I do when I arrive at the Benavides' house is to fill my lungs with that fragrance. Through the Spanish doorway, you go down a flight of steps into a triangular courtyard. Two sides of it are walled off by the house. The other is smothered in flowers and vines, with another flight of steps leading up to Felipe's lovingly maintained replica of an English pub complete with horse brasses, old-fashioned car horns and little tables made out of beer barrels sliced in two.

We reminisced on the terrace until two in the morning and then Marie Louise showed us to our suite. In our bedroom, on the dressing table just under the window, was a large ripe banana.

'Is that in case we get hungry?' asked John.

'No, no,' Marie Louise chuckled. 'It's for the night monkey. He usually comes every night and knocks on the window for his banana.'

She kissed us goodnight. 'By the way,' she said as an afterthought, 'if we should happen to have an earthquake at night, this is what you should do. If it's not a very bad one, go down to the shelter under the staircase. If it is a very bad one, go out into the garden.'

We couldn't work out how to tell whether an earthquake was bad or not but we were much too exhausted to think about it. My head hit the pillow and I fell into a deep sleep at once but I was awakened not long after by a tap-tap-tap at the window. There, saucer-eyed in the dark, was the douroucouli, the night monkey. I hastened to give him what he had come for – his banana.

The following day we drove out to visit the zoo run by Felipe's sister, Carmen. We learned a good deal there about the trials and tribulations of running a zoo in Peru. The zoo was outside Lima in an area dotted with the ruins of pre-Inca civilisations. Unfortunately Carmen suffered the consequences of the perennial food shortages in Lima, where at that time you were only permitted to buy meat during one half of the month.

'You have to understand what we're up against,' said Carmen, a small, auburn-haired woman totally devoted to her animals. 'I can't blame the keepers because people are poor here, and even if they have money it's hard to buy what you need. But if we give meat to the keepers to feed to the big cats they will put it out on the plates for the animals and then, when no one is looking, hide it and take it home for their families. And when we give them milk for the baby monkeys, often enough they'll drink it or take that home as well. It's terrible, but what can one do?'

The problem that Carmen faced with her zoo was really typical of South America as a whole: the idea of animal conservation is still alien to most people. The common habit of mind is that anything that walks on all fours is meant for the cooking pot. I asked Carmen whether she could not find time to come to Europe and visit Kilverstone. She said that she would love to but that when she had risked taking a single weekend off – her only break in many years – a friend had telephoned to tell her that in her absence none of her animals had been fed. She had had to go flying back.

There were a number of curiosities in her zoo. I found some Peruvian hairless dogs there; previously, I had thought that hairless dogs were unique to Mexico. They were quite the ugliest dogs I have ever seen and they came in all sorts of colours – grey, pink, charcoal. The Incas used them as hot-water bottles. She had some round, tubby pacaranas, one of the rarest members of the rodent family, looking exactly like rats that someone had puffed up with a bicycle pump. Carmen also had some emperor marmosets with long white whiskers just like the Emperor Franz Josef. I was very jealous of them. And she had a pair of the hideous, bald ukari monkeys, sometimes called 'the Englishmen' in South America because of their bright pink faces. The ukari is the only New World monkey whose tail is shorter than its head and body. To me they were quite the ugliest things that I had seen on my trip to Peru but they would leap into Carmen's arms and display slobbery affection. Beauty is only skin deep.

At Carmen's zoo we also saw for the first time the spectacled bear, the only South American bear, named after the white splodges around its eyes that make it look as if it is wearing glasses. Felipe Benavides is a great champion of the spectacled bear, which is today an endangered species. His concern for the spectacled bear has brought him into conflict with some powerful people, most notably a brother of the Shah of Persia who was given a permit by the Peruvian government to shoot the spectacled bear and the equally rare Andean deer. Felipe created a scandal out of the episode, getting university students and Boy Scouts to raise a petition to the government to preserve the spectacled bear, regardless of who it was who wanted to hunt it. He chalked up a notable triumph: he prevented the Shah's brother from shooting the spectacled bear although I gather that he did get a crack at the Andean deer. The idea of anyone killing members of an endangered species merely in order to put a stuffed head on their wall makes me quite sick.

The following day we drove up into the high Andes above Arequipa, to a reserve that Felipe had created for vicuñas. We saw five separate herds. In each one there was a dominant male who was surrounded by numerous females and who had to fight off the younger bucks who wanted to challenge his patriarchal rights. Higher up, in the midst of a snowstorm at about 15,000 feet, we saw Andean geese, the majestic condors overhead and great mounds of bright green moss in the midst of a desolate, rocky terrain where the chinchilla-like mountain viscacha lives. The height left me breathless and headachy. It was a great relief to start back on our descent.

On the way down, crossing the altiplano, or high plateau, we passed by a salt lake about twelve miles long. Stretched across its centre was a line of bright pink flamingos about three miles long. Nearby we found huge herds of alpacas with tufts of red wool plaited on to the ends of their ears, probably because a feast day was looming up and the shepherds wanted them to look festive.

We were travelling through Inca country. The Incas were great agriculturalists, expert in irrigation and the terracing of mountain slopes in order to conserve the soil that would otherwise have been washed away. Before the Spanish colonists arrived they grew all sorts of plants, including twenty varieties of maize, forty varieties of potatoes, sweet potatoes, squashes, beans, manioc, tapioca, peanuts, cashew nuts, avocados, tomatoes, peppers and maté. One of their inventions was freeze-drying: the Indians of the Andes were the first producers of powdered mashed potato. They would lay out their potatoes, which would freeze overnight and go mushy the following day as they thawed out. In the morning the Inca farmers would trample the mush and squeeze out the water. Repeating the process every day for a week, they would produce a dried pulp which could be stored against hungry times.

When we returned to Felipe's villa we found that the night monkey who had visited us the first day had become our faithful friend. Felipe and Marie Louise called him Happy because of his habit of grinning with his mouth open while making a very human-sounding chuckling noise. Happy, we found, was becoming too good a friend. By the time we left he had taken to coming and rattling on the window-pane three times a night. He would come in the early evening, again about midnight and yet again in the early hours of the morning.

One evening I had gone to have a bath before dressing for dinner. I crawled into the bath in the dark with my watch on. I did not turn the light on because I thought that Happy would not come if the electric bulb was blazing. I quite forgot about the watch which was not, unfortunately, one of those ultra-modern waterproof jobs, and I squealed when I realised that I had probably ruined the mechanism, not for the first time. As I jumped out of the bath to try to dry the watch out, I saw Happy hopping back into the bushes.

Felipe reproached me later on the grounds that I had been a corrupting influence on Happy. After John and I left, the night monkey went on calling on Felipe and Marie Louise three or even four times a night. In an effort to allow themselves some sleep, they rigged up a sort of gangplank leading from the window-grille to the top of their four-poster bed where they would place a bowl of fruit. They did not put the fruit on the window-sill – which would seem the most obvious thing to do – because they feared that the ants would arrive before Happy.

One night, the bed started shaking violently.

'Terremoto, terremoto!' shouted Felipe. 'Earthquake, earthquake!' They jumped out of bed and grabbed for the light switch.

Looking back from the doorway as he prepared to dash out into the garden, Felipe saw Happy sitting atop the four-poster, shaking himself vigorously. You would never think that a harmless, ruminative creature like a douroucouli could put someone in mind of an earthquake.

That was not the end of the troubles that my love-affair with Happy, the night monkey, had bequeathed to the Benavides. Not long after, Marie Louise awoke with a start, convinced that she was being eaten alive by fleas. When Felipe turned on the lights, they found that an army of ants had taken advantage of Happy's gangplank. After feasting on the monkey's bowl of fruit they had decided to drop in on Felipe and Marie Louise for a little human companionship. Needless to say it was I who was blamed for turning an unassertive little night creature into a ravening glutton who disrupted the hours of darkness.

11

Ellie Ocelot and Others

While Rudolf and Mrs Wolf were starting their stormy career and Nickit was the baby of the house, we had two new arrivals at Kilverstone. Our friends, Nate and Ellie Gale, wrote to us from Panama to ask whether we would like to have an ocelot and a baby margay like the one I had seen on Ellie's kitchen window-sill. The animals were the orphans of American servicemen who had kept them as pets while they were stationed in the Canal Zone but were not permitted to take them back to the United States. Naturally I wrote back by return to say that we would be delighted to give them a new home.

John at once set about building them cages on the west-facing wall beside the otters. Each cage had its own pond since, contrary to what many people imagine, South American wild cats love to play about in the water.

The ocelot is called the *chibi-guazu*, or 'big cat', by the Indians of Paraguay and the one that arrived from Panama, an enchanting ball of spotted fluff, was not much bigger than a kitten. We called her Ellie after our friend. Ellie the ocelot was very friendly, and when she came out of quarantine she would gambol about and rub herself against me like an affectionate pussy.

As Ellie grew bigger she turned into a striking beauty and was an instant hit on television. We received a flood of mail after Ellie's debut on the 'Animal Magic' programme, during which she presented first one profile, then the other, to the camera with the fake insouciance of a pin-up girl.

But Ellie, as we soon learned, was equally capable of throwing a tantrum worthy of a prima donna if she got bored with rehearsals. 'Animal Magic' invited Ellie to make a return appearance the following week, under pressure from the instant fan club that she seemed to have acquired. They wanted to put her in a glass-walled enclosure with a tree for her to climb. She behaved impeccably during the first rehearsal, climbing the tree and displaying her profile to the cameraman as if she had been modelling all her life. But during the second rehearsal she began to show tell-tale signs of boredom, testing the height of the glass wall with her paws. And when it came to doing the live show she impetuously leaped out of her enclosure and raced across the studio, apparently in search of the baby badgers in the next set. The cameras tracked her helplessly and presented a first-class view of a retreating tail. Ellie, alas, had wrecked her budding career as a television star. She was not asked back.

If you can't make it in the movies, you might as well try for a quiet married life. We found a mate for Ellie called Oscar, who turned out to be a wild, spitting ball of fire. You have to be very careful about how you introduce wild cats to each other. If you simply thrust a male and a female into the same cage without complicated introductions, the chances are that they will fly at each other and that one of them will be killed. So all our cat houses at Kilverstone are very carefully constructed with separate bedrooms for the male and the female and a grille in between so that they can get to know each other before they are able to get at each other. It was only after two weeks of sniffing and eyeing each other that Ellie and Oscar were allowed out to meet in the main part of the cage.

Ellie and Oscar seemed to treat their relationship like an arranged marriage. They had strong differences of opinion – over humans, for example. Ellie seemed to miss her games with me and would come sidling up to the edge of her cage, purring softly, whenever I approached. Oscar, however, did not have much time for humans. I thought I had better not contribute to their marital squabbles so I kept pretty much apart from Ellie now, although I would often stop and tickle her through the weld mesh of the cage.

When Ellie was about two years old I sat down one day on the bottom rail of the barrier outside her cage with a baby spider monkey on my lap. I played with Ellie for a while and was just getting up to leave when a woman visitor came up to ask me about the baby monkey. Sitting with my arms crossed a foot or so from the cage, I forgot about Ellie and Oscar as we chatted away. While I was looking the other way, Oscar slunk up to the edge of the cage, shot his paw through the mesh and pulled my hand through. I was surprised by his strength. I was more than surprised when he started to chew on my finger as if it were an old bone. Blood poured out and I started to scream blue murder.

'Are you all right?' asked the visitor, as if this was a normal occurrence.

'For God's sake, call a keeper!' I pleaded.

Stuart bobbed his head out of the keeper's kitchen and vanished inside, re-emerging with a dead, day-old chick that he must have thought would tempt Oscar to abandon my finger. But this ploy didn't work. Oscar's attitude seemed to be that he was not going to give up a tasty bit of steak for a scrawny bird. Instead of getting a stick to push Oscar away, on the spur of the moment Stuart grabbed hold of my hand and wrenched it back, out of Oscar's mouth. But not all of my finger came with it: nearly all of the flesh of the index finger on my right hand, down to the base of the nail, had stayed in Oscar's mouth.

When I got to the plastic surgeon, heavily drugged, about

an hour and a half later, I heard him saying, 'Where's the rest of your finger? I can sew it back on.'

'Oh, it's in Oscar's stomach,' I groaned.

'Who's Oscar?' he asked in amazement.

'A very jealous husband,' I heard myself say.

It was only when I came out of my drugged state later on that I thought to explain to the surgeon that Oscar was an ocelot.

'I'm terribly relieved to hear it,' he said. 'I had been looking at Lord Fisher rather strangely.'

When Ellie the ocelot arrived we were just finishing the Burrowing House. This is a large, darkened hall with five burrows – double bedrooms topped with glass – around three of its walls. The public can peer, like Peeping Toms, into the homes of badgers, two kinds of agoutis and viscachas, the burrowers of the New World.

The viscachas, which live in large herds in the Argentine pampas, are particularly piratical-looking rodents with two wide bands across their faces like a mask. We soon found that life is pretty rough for male viscachas as the females have a vicious temper and drive their spouses away when they have fulfilled their matrimonial duties, even to the extent of trying to deny them food. We had a very formidable female who managed to dispose of several mates shortly before producing her litters. How she accomplished this was, rather a mystery: there were no bite-marks on the males' corpses and in any case they were bigger and stronger than the female and should have been able to defend themselves. How did the males die? We sought the advice of Chester Zoo in our efforts to solve this whodunnit. They found that the same thing had happened to some of their male viscachas.

The only theory that seemed to account for this trail of corpses was that the female viscacha compensated for her physical inferiority to the male by sheer forcefulness of character – after all, that pattern is not entirely unfamiliar in human families! – and succeeded after mating in starving her spouse to death by keeping him away from food. Whether or not we had found the right answer, we did find a way to ensure a longer life for our henpecked male viscachas. We would separate them from the females after the mating sessions as soon as they began to look a little the worse for wear.

Surprisingly in view of its diminutive size, the viscacha will attack humans if it is taken by surprise, letting out an ear-piercing noise like a screech in an old horror film. We kept our first viscachas in the stables while the Burrowing House was being built. One day I was in the stables, clearing wood to make room for some new animals, when I was startled by a blood-curdling scream and dropped some logs on my toes. The noise came from a viscacha who had got out of the next-door stable, was under the pile of logs I was moving and seemed bent on trying to take a bite out of me. I had to drive it away with a broom handle.

Next door to the viscachas in the Burrowing House we kept black and orange-rumped agoutis. The agouti looks like a large, tail-less rat but is not nearly so aggressive and is one hundred per cent vegetarian. Our first pair came from Lima Zoo. They bred enthusiastically and we soon had a large tribe. They have an extraordinary gnawing capacity and are capable of drilling a hole through a nut half an inch thick.

The badgers in the Burrowing House are intruders since they came from England, not the New World. But I have a special fondness for them because I reared them myself after they were given to me by a friend. When they were small I would take them about the park with me every afternoon and they would frisk about at my heels like puppies. Baby badgers instinctively follow their parents nose to tail and they would trot along in the same way at my heel. When they grew up and moved to the Burrowing House they reverted to being primarily nocturnal creatures.

The children who visit Kilverstone find the Burrowing House a spooky place. The darkness is relieved only by the reddish light from the burrows, which is designed not to disturb the sleeping animals. I don't think it will be the last home for my badgers. I think I will take them down to my house in Sussex and release them there to live in the bluebell woods where Kipling wrote his tales of the Marklake witches.

The most combative animals at Kilverstone are the tayras. The tayra is a member of the weasel family, but ours look rather like old roués, complete with moustaches, winged collars and spats. They are full of nervous energy and will spend a lot of time streaking round and round their cage. If they decide to attack a human they do it in earnest and their classic line of attack is to hurl themselves at the chest and then climb up towards the throat in an effort to sink their teeth into it.

We bought a third tayra from another zoo to join the pair of females we had already brought to Kilverstone. We soon found out that the new tayra had been wrongly sexed; it was also a female. We thought we would smooth the introduction of the new animal by tying its cage next to that of the other tayras so that they could smell and see each other but not come into physical contact. That way we hoped to reduce the risk of a fight; it would be normal enough for our existing tayras to defend their territory by attacking a complete stranger.

After three weeks we thought it would be safe enough to introduce the new resident. But the longer-established pair wouldn't hear of it. They flew for the new tayra with teeth and claws and they would no doubt have inflicted some severe injuries on each other if Brian and Keith had not intervened. They thrust themselves into the middle of the cage, brandishing lumps of wood in their hands. Somehow they managed to grab hold of the tails of the two older tayras and heaved them into a den in the side of the cage that could be cut off by a heavy slide. Brian was just starting to mop his brow when he saw the new tayra that they had been trying to protect flying like a missile at Keith's chest. She had been pretty badly cut up and obviously thought that Brian and Keith were on the side of her attackers.

Not long after I lost the top of my finger to Oscar the ocelot, John had his own run-in with a tayra. He was working on extending a wall and was gripping the top of the wall of the tayras' enclosure. While his fingers were hanging there, one of the tayras leaped at his hand and took a savage bite at it.

'I've joined the club,' he said to me afterwards, enigmatically.

'Oh really, darling? Do you mean White's?'

'No, the Finger Club,' he said ruefully, holding up a bandaged forefinger.

12

Jubilee the Jaguar

Few animals in a zoo are as exciting as the big cats, or as beautiful to watch in motion. The jaguar rules the jungle of South America and has made its home in all the territories between Arizona and Argentina. Its throaty roar, like hoarse coughing – a series of 'uh, uh, uh' sounds coming louder and faster – sends every other animal and bird in the forest scuttling away in panic. Indian hunters sometimes try to imitate the sound with a wooden trumpet. The jaguar's name is derived from an Indian word, *yaquara*, that means 'he who kills with one leap'. The name fits: the jaguar rarely needs to leap more than once after it has crept up on its prey, its tail swishing from side to side in a movement that is said to hypnotise its victims. The jaguar will kill with a single blow from its mighty paw or by tearing its victim's throat out with its cruel teeth.

The jaguar resembles the leopard but is much more sturdily built, with a barrel of a chest and a short, muscular neck. Its spots are larger than those of the leopard, like rosettes with a smaller black spot at the centre. The jaguar has stronger teeth than the lion or the tiger. And although it cannot match the tiger in size, the jaguar can weigh more than 300 lb. The male is often more than six feet long and some jaguars have been sighted in the wild that were said to have been half as long again.

It is not surprising that the Indian peoples of the New World have traditionally approached this splendid, dangerous beast with its huge, gold-flecked eyes with a religious awe. The shamans and witch-doctors of jungle tribes still wear the jaguar-skin and are believed to be men into whom the jaguar's soul has entered. Hunters mix a few jaguar hairs into their curare bowls as a supernatural assurance that the poison will work and the arrows strike their target.

In ancient Mexico the people of the Zapotec culture raised a citadel in honour of the Jaguar God at Monte Alban. Earlier devotees of the Jaguar God went to the extreme of deforming their children's heads in imitation of the animal's flattened skull. Fanatics preserved these traditions after the Spanish conquest, practising the secret and bloody cult of the 'Jaguar People' – the Nahualistas – who carried out ferocious ritual murders dressed in jaguar skins.

The Mayas, the vanished philosopher-kings of Central America, depicted the jaguar and the crocodile supporting the world on their shoulders. They raised a magnificent Temple of the Jaguars among the stepped pyramids of their city at Chichen-Itza, whose ruins survive in the depths of the jungle. The jaguar was worshipped by the Incas and the peoples they conquered as well.

In its own environment the jaguar need fear only man. A jaguar can usually beat a giant anaconda, a cayman or a puma, although very occasionally one is torn to shreds by a herd of wild peccaries, hog-like animals which are only about twenty inches high but have razor-sharp hooves. But now the human hunters are a threat to the survival of the jaguar. Once, they came to kill it because they thought it would devour their cattle herds. Now they come to hunt the jaguar, like the other spotted cats, to provide skins for ladies' coats. It is a scandal that the traffic goes on, and yet, even if the laws were changed throughout South America, the sale of skins has become a million-dollar business and it would be very hard to track down poachers along the wild southern and western borders of Brazil.

We were very anxious to find a pair of these extraordinary animals for Kilverstone and if possible to breed from them. We were told that a man with a private zoo in Weybridge, Surrey, had a pair of jaguars that he wanted to sell and we duly set off to have a look at them. The animals were kept in the spacious gardens of a rambling mock-Elizabethan villa that belonged to one of the entrepreneurs of pop music who had made his fortune by managing some of the best-known teen idols of the 'sixties. He had decided to keep gorillas and big cats. It might sound like a gimmick to amuse his pop star friends but in fact he had a magnificent collection, superbly kept in airy, immaculately clean cages with plenty of space to roam round.

The jaguars had been christened Jason and Josephine. Jason was a strapping four-year-old, much bigger than average, with a magnificent coat of an ochre colour. He had been bred in Chester Zoo and was obviously in peak condition. As he loped around the cage we decided at once that we must have him. Josephine was a rather different proposition. She was an elderly female, worn out by the years she had been kept in a circus, with a stomach that dragged along the ground and made her always look as if she was pregnant. We guessed that she was no longer capable of breeding and wondered whether she would really fit in at Kilverstone. However, their owner was determined to sell both or neither, so we agreed to buy Josephine as well to keep Jason company while we looked for a younger female.

We put them into their cage among the cherry trees. We had been warned of the danger of over-feeding predators in captivity – after all, they have to hunt for food in the wild and may spend days between kills. So we arranged for one day of fasting every week. On the other days we fed the jaguars whole rabbits and pigeons as well as big slabs of beef so that they could crunch their way through the fur and feathers and bones as they would do in the wild; jaguars tend to lick their meat off the bones with their great rough tongues rather than chew it. A very few zoos feed live animals to their big cats as a partial substitute for the joys of the chase that are denied them in captivity but we couldn't bring ourselves to do this.

We soon found that we had guessed right about Josephine. Jason would frequently approach her amorously but she would fly at him with teeth and claws, sending the fur flying. She was a 'not tonight, Josephine' type. She was not merely playing hard to get. The vet discovered that she had stomach cancer and we reluctantly agreed to have her put down. .

We were able to find Jason a more suitable bride – a nubile young female of the same yellow-reddish hue whom we christened Jenny. We kept her in a separate pen for the first two days while we watched carefully to see how Jason would receive her. Jaguars are notoriously anti-social in the wild. In captivity a male has been known to maul and even bite to death an alien female that was too suddenly introduced. But within two days Jason was purring happily at Jenny and we decided it was safe to put them together. Through the summer they romped about together or reclined in lazy splendour on the logs we had set among the blossoming cherry trees in their cage. When they began to mate they announced it to all their animal neighbours by raising a terrific din. The acrid, musky odour of their cage became even stronger.

In the spring of the Queen's Jubilee year, 1977, Jenny produced two cubs. One was still-born. The other entered the world as a tiny dark hairy ball with its eyes tightly shut – jaguars are born blind and do not open their eyes for at least two weeks after birth.

After watching mother and baby for ten days we became worried that Jenny was not producing enough milk to feed her baby. With some misgivings John agreed that I should take it inside the house. Jason and Jenny seemed unperturbed and mated again almost immediately.

That summer the country was full of flags and processions as the British people, divided over so many things, came together to celebrate the Jubilee of the world's best-loved Sovereign. Naturally we decided that our jaguar cub, which turned out to be a female, had to be called Jubilee. I put her into a little basket by my bed. As she grew bigger she was transferred to a laundry basket. I fed her on Lactol (a special milk for cats) every three hours, day and night. When she was three weeks old she measured just seventeen inches from the tip of her nose to the root of her tail and weighed only 5 lb. 3 oz.

Her first, hesitant movements were a sort of breast-stroke; her little legs could hardly keep her tummy off the ground. Her first playmate, inevitably, was Tia the chihuahua who after all her experiences with the baby monkeys was by now starting to see herself as a mother to everything that lived and breathed. In their gambols around the sitting-room Jubilee started practising her jumps by leaping up on to tables and cupboards.

Tia actually seemed to be more in control of Jubilee than I was. As Jubilee got bigger, Tia would growl at her if she misbehaved. If that didn't work Tia would grab her ear and shake her as hard as she could. This method of discipline proved infallible for the whole time Jubilee was with her. Perhaps it is not as surprising as it sounds: baby jaguars need a lot of mothering in the wild until they reach maturity at the age of about eighteen months. They have to learn how to jump and swim and stalk their prey and they tend to stick close to their mothers until then. But Jubilee took no notice of my scoldings, even if I gave her a cuff like her real mother would do with her paw.

Each day she came for a walk with me through the park, sometimes on a collar and leash, more often gambolling along at my heel. These walks were a great adventure for her.

When we got to the paddocks where the miniature horses were kept, she practised stalking them through the grass, her little nose twitching and her tail waving from side to side. Jubilee got quite a fright when she got right up to the nose of Evita who, though only twenty-seven inches tall, was still several times as big as she was.

Jubilee had longer outings. We took her to London and to Bristol to appear on television and even to Ascot. I felt nervous about what the stewards at the Royal Enclosure would think about a baby jaguar coming to the races so I kept her tucked away in her basket in the car. I missed the Gold Cup rushing back and forth to give her her bottle and check that she was all right.

I weighed Jubilee at Kilverstone every Sunday. We started off using the kitchen scales, but by the time she was about four months old we had to progress to an Edwardian set of jockey's scales that were kept in a store room upstairs. She was getting too heavy for me to bundle about on my own so I asked John to help me get her on to the scales. Afterwards we took her down to the kitchen to measure her length and height. Just as I was getting out the tape-measure, Jubilee spied one of my sandals and pounced on it, striking it with her paw and gnawing at it and worrying it about as if she was trying to kill it. She became very excited and dragged the sandal through the orangery. We ran in behind her. She dashed behind a chair and then, as we stood waiting for her to calm down, she shot out from behind the chair and sank her teeth and claws into John's leg. John seized her by the scruff of her neck and wrenched her off. He was wearing thick jeans so the cuts were not very deep, but we realised that a bite like that would have put paid to Tia; it was a warning signal that Jubilee was growing up.

None of the big cats can be truly domesticated. They are not built to be house-pets and the jaguar is the least easily tamed of all. There are legends in South America of big cats that have befriended man but it has to be on their terms, not ours.

I scooped up Jubilee and thrust her into her basket. 'Oh dear,' I said to her. 'You know what happens when you bite John.'

Within half an hour I took Jubilee down to the park. She had calmed down completely and trotted along at my heel like a dog. We put her into a cage of her own as it would have been dangerous to put her back into her parents' cage after an absence of four months. They might not have recognised her and in any case, cat fathers are often none too gentle with their young: they tend to be indifferent when they are not murderously hostile. One dealer we know told us of an incident when a male serval cat stretched its paw through the wire, pulled its cub through and killed it.

Fortunately Jason showed more paternal instinct when two more cubs were born to Jenny in October of that year. We never allowed them to be together until one of the cubs stretched its paw through the wire of Jason's pen and he licked it in a friendly way. Even then we didn't allow them to be in the same cage as him without close supervision at first.

Every time I visited her, Jubilee showed off the skills she had been developing by herself, leaping about the cage and darting among the branches. One day Tia, probably alarmed by the size of 'baby', growled at her from the other side of the wire. Jubilee slunk to the back of the cage as if to say, 'What have I done wrong now?'

13

An Argentinian Shark

My passion for the miniature horses got us involved in our first experience of the Latin American con-trick. I don't suppose that Latin Americans are any more or less honest in their business dealings, on the whole, than most other people. John and I had been very lucky to have made good friends in most of the Latin American countries where we travelled to find animals for Kilverstone, who shepherded us away from the inevitable community of sharks and con-men. But my love of the little horses and my eagerness to breed them at our own park led us into a snare that, as I could see later, common sense should have told us to avoid.

I had read that at the Falabella stud in Argentina they had bred horses less than twenty inches high. I wrote twice to Señor Falabella to inquire whether he had any for sale that we would be able to breed from. Weeks passed and there was still no reply. So we consulted the Economic Minister at the Argentine Embassy in London who supplied us with the name of an Argentine dealer who might be able to help us.

I began a seemingly endless correspondence with this dealer, whom I shall call Juan Goldmann. He wrote on imposing notepaper, assuring us that he could sell us horses that were only twenty inches high. It was finally agreed that he would send us two miniature palominos called Napoleon and Elba. Then the first snag came up. We had nearly settled everything when Sr Goldmann sent me a letter in which he mentioned, in a nonchalant postscript, that the stallion had been castrated and that there would obviously be no chance of breeding from this pair. Bitterly disappointed, I wrote back saying that I wasn't interested in castrated animals. The whole point of our zoo was that we wanted to breed different species and, after all, the thing that people most want to see when they come to Kilverstone are the baby animals. It is horrible to me to think of depriving animals of the pleasure of having babies.

Sr Goldmann wrote again to say that if I wanted a pair of horses that would breed I would have to fork out an extra $2,000 for each one – a pretty stiff price on top of the $4,000 a head that he had demanded in the first place. But if we were prepared to buy four horses instead of two, he went on, we could have a small discount. To tempt me with this offer, he enclosed a photograph of a beautiful little spotted horse that I quite fell in love with.

This led to much heart-rending and some earnest consultations with the bank manager. Because John was struggling to make ends meet at the park, I had said that I would pay for the horses out of a little nest-egg that I had kept tucked away. I tried to justify to the bank manager my love affair with the spotted horse that I had only seen in a photograph by arguing that he would be a tremendous draw-card and that thousands more people would come to Kilverstone just to see such an unusual creature – which, indeed, we were convinced they would.

With a twinkle in his eye he said, 'I can see there's no way of stopping you.'

I wrote to Sr Goldmann straight away, asking for a pair of tiny palominos and a pair of spotted Falabellas. I was rather surprised by his next letter. He told me that I would have to transfer the full purchase price in American dollars to his bank in the United States before the horses were delivered. In the meantime, he said, he would not even be able to send me a photograph of my horses. He gave me a long-winded explanation for this, claiming that because the stud was many miles outside Buenos Aires, it would take time to arrange a visit by a professional photographer and that there were further complications because it was difficult to get colour film developed in Argentina.

I suppose I should have smelled a rat at this stage. But, short of making a special trip to Argentina at a time when both of us were tied up with feeding and housing lots of new arrivals, as well as preparing for the summer rush of visitors to the park, I did not see any other way of getting the horses. So with some rumbling misgivings, I had the money transferred to Sr Goldmann's bank in March 1977.

He had solemnly assured me that the horses would be dispatched within fifteen days of payment but for many weeks I heard absolutely nothing. I became very worried that the mysterious Sr Goldmann had decided to do a moonlight flit. In between brooding about how on earth we could track Sr Goldmann down if he had really decided to abscond, I became very angry at the thought that we might not have the horses in time for the next season's visitors. A zoo, like a cinema or a theatre, is always in need of new attractions if it has to pay its own way.

Sr Goldmann surfaced again in May, when he wrote to say that he had got his money but delivery of the horses was being delayed by the fact that he had had to send blood samples to Britain and had so far failed to get any response. This story sounded about as plausible as his essay on colour photography in Argentina. We checked around and soon discovered that none of the likely authorities had received any blood samples. 'You don't need to send them anyway,' one official informed us.

'I'm afraid, darling, that you've been had,' John concluded at this point. 'Do we know any lawyers in Buenos Aires?'

'Well, I'm not giving up yet,' I insisted. 'Weren't you the first one to tell me about the mañana complex?'

Many mañanas came and went.

It was not until the end of summer that we heard that the first pair of horses, the palominos, were ready for dispatch. They were to be flown across by British Caledonian but the airline rang us to say that they were worried that there was not enough air circulating in the holds of their planes to keep the horses alive on the long flight from Buenos Aires. The horses would have to be sent some other way. This should have been a job for Sr Goldmann but he seemed to think that he had now fulfilled his side of the contract. After much chasing around airline offices, I settled on Lufthansa, who seemed happy enough to have Falabellas as passengers.

With a long sigh of relief, I got down to giving a last coat of paint to the fences round the paddocks which we had set aside for our new arrivals. Suddenly, I remembered a conversation I had had with Michael Brambell, the curator of mammals at London Zoo.

'I envy you getting your Falabellas,' he had remarked. 'We had very much wanted to get some for London Zoo a few years back. In fact we had actually put them on board a ship. But the ship docked at an African port and they are so frightened of importing animal diseases from Africa to this country that when the ship got to Britain, the health inspectors stopped us from taking the horses off. We had to send them back.'

It suddenly struck me that what had happened to London Zoo could happen to us. What if the plane stopped for refuelling somewhere in Africa? I was so agitated that I dropped my paintbrush on my foot and tore inside to ring up Lufthansa to check.

'Well, Madam,' said the polite voice, 'we do stop in Dakar.'

I was so flustered that for a moment I couldn't remember where Dakar was. Surely he couldn't mean Bengal? No, of course not. Senegal.

'But you can't go to Senegal,' I protested.

'I'm sorry, madam, but that's what's in the flight schedule.'

I explained the difficulty. The Lufthansa man said reassuringly that he was certain no problem would arise. After all, the plane only stopped to refuel. The hold would not be opened.

Alas, the man at the Ministry of Agriculture thought differently when I called afterwards to check. It seemed that if the wheels of the plane so much as grazed the tarmac of an African airfield we would not be allowed to bring the horses into Britain.

Since the horses were supposed to leave Buenos Aires within twenty-four hours I rang Lufthansa back in a great flap to cancel the flight. I spent the rest of the day on the telephone, trying to find an airline that would bring the horses from Buenos Aires without touching down anywhere in Africa. I thought I had found the answer when I got on to Pan Am. Yes, Pan Am could take the horses via the United States.

'But you do realise,' the girl warned, 'that there will be a delay for at least a day in New York so the health authorities can conduct a blood test.'

After all the delays we had had to put up with, one day more did not sound too forbidding.

'What happens,' I asked innocently, 'if for some reason their blood tests are not up to scratch?'

'Oh, the standard procedure is for the animals to be shot on the spot.'

'Thank you *very* much!' I said, slamming down the receiver. There must be a better way than that for my Falabellas to travel.

Of course, I should have thought of it to begin with. What about their own national airlines, Aerolineas Argentinas? Yes, Aerolineas could provide a direct flight from Buenos Aires to Madrid, skipping Africa. Just one teeny-weeny problem: the personnel at Madrid airport were on strike, on top of a go-slow at Heathrow. This had to be it.

After another wait and several more telexes to Sr Goldmann, we had a flight number and a time of arrival. The horses were really coming. We drove down to London to spend the night with my daughter, Trina, and her husband, and then headed out to Heathrow at the crack of dawn to pick up the horses. I had a shock in store.

The horses were not palominos and they were certainly not nineteen and a half inches high. The male was a fawnish colour all over and the female was vaguely chestnutty. They were both about twenty-seven inches high and they looked distinctly wan.

'The stallion looks completely knackered,' said John. He didn't realise then how accurate this observation would prove to be.

I was desperately upset. It was obvious that we had been conned and I felt an utter fool, especially since I knew that the press and television people were waiting to see the horses, which we had all expected to be the smallest in the country.

'Can't you just put them back on the plane and send them back where they came from?' I asked the man from Aerolineas. I was on the edge of bursting into tears.

He made a gesture of infinite understanding and infinite helplessness. It was a less than brilliant idea. It had cost us £800 to bring the horses over so it would presumably cost us another £800 to send them back – plus room and board while they rested before the return flight. Would we ever get any of this money back, let alone the right horses, from the elusive Sr Goldmann? There was simply no way of knowing.

So ruefully we packed the horses into the back of our Kilverstone van and drove them over to my sister's house, Barkham Manor, to spend the night. They had an appointment the following day to be photographed with the King's Troop of the Royal Horse Artillery.

'The best thing is to put a brave face on it,' said John. 'We can't call the press off at this stage and anyway the chances are that no one will notice what's happened.'

When I saw our horses in the park the following day, cantering beside the splendid mounts of the King's Troop or posing for the photographers between their legs, almost overshadowed even by my small granddaughter, Pandora, I started to think that things were not so bad. The Falabellas looked so small and so fragile beside the horses of the King's Troop that it seemed unlikely that any pressman would be beady-eyed enough to spot that they were seven inches taller than they were supposed to be.

Never underrate the press. The phone calls started coming in that afternoon.

'Excuse me for saying this, Lady Fisher,' said the first reporter, 'but your horses seem to be bigger than we were led to expect.'

I had to admit that we had been sent the wrong ones.

'I'm not trying to make a pun, but don't you think you were taken for a ride?'

'Well, yes, I'm afraid it does look rather like that.'

A television crew came up to Kilverstone from London that night to film the whole story. I suppose there is nothing that people enjoy so much as hearing about someone else being taken for a sucker. If the sucker happens to have a title, the story is even more entertaining. I'm not complaining about this: as it turned out, the spate of publicity on television and in the newspapers brought hundreds of letters of sympathy from all over the world and a throng of curious spectators to the park.

One embarrassment was that we had made a number of Argentine friends including Edgardo Segura, the charming Naval Attaché at the Embassy in London, and some of the press accounts made it sound as if we had been conned through some fault of the Embassy. In a sense this was true; the Embassy had recommended Sr Goldmann to us in the first place. But I certainly didn't want to appear to be blaming Embassy officials – they were as horrified by Sr Goldmann's business methods as we were.

A few weeks after the horses, now christened Argentina and Chico, had arrived, we were due to go to a party at the Argentine Embassy in Belgrave Square. I was more depressed than ever about the horses. Argentina had arrived very sickly and we had had to send her repeatedly to the equine research station at Newmarket. She spent a solid two weeks there on one occasion, being nursed back to health. The medical research people at Newmarket, fortunately for us, were delighted to have such exotic horses to examine. But they had bad news for us about Chico, the little stallion: they told us that he was incapable of breeding since his testicles had not descended.

'You were right about him looking knackered,' I conceded glumly to John.

Sr Goldmann had conned us again. I had had to fork out an extra $4,000 for a pair of Falabellas that would breed and he had sent me a stallion that simply wasn't up to the job. I fired off another furious letter. But would we ever get the horses we had been promised?

Despite my black mood, I was nervous rather than angry on the night of the Argentine Embassy party.

'Oh dear,' I said to John as we got into our old blue canvas-topped Bentley to drive to the Embassy. 'Do you suppose Edgardo saw us on television? It will be awfully embarrassing if he thinks that we're blaming it all on the Embassy.'

'I don't know whether that would be such a bad thing. It might prod them into doing something to get us the right horses. There must be some laws in Argentina to prevent this sort of thing happening.'

Still, I was very jittery when we arrived at the Embassy and took our place in the reception line. I was wearing an organza dress and kind of belt made from crystal beads. I couldn't stop fidgeting with the belt. As an immense major-domo in a bright red jacket and an almost equally ruddy face boomed out 'Lord and Lady Fisher', I gave the belt an almighty tug. John said afterwards that it was a yank which could have pulled the *Queen Mary* from her moorings. I pulled so hard that the belt broke and the crystal beads went cascading in all directions over the spendid marble floor, rolling under the feet of the guests, the waiters and the Embassy officials who were lined up to greet us. Worst of all, the beads sounded like a machine-gun fire as they hit the marble. One naval officer, obviously thinking that terrorists had struck, wheeled round so abruptly that he spilled his drink down the front of a diplomat's wife.

'Good God!' I exclaimed at the top of my voice, quite involuntarily. I clasped both my hands to my waist, trying to save as many beads as I could.

John grabbed me and dragged me out of the queue and back into the outer lobby where I tried to knot the belt so that no more beads would escape. The Argentians took it with great good humour. For the rest of the evening, the major-domo kept coming up with handfuls of beads.

'I see you are taking your revenge,' joked Edgardo, the Naval Attaché. 'What will you do to us next? Obviously the Embassy is going to be in ruins unless we can solve your problem.'

I peered uneasily about the room over the top of my glass, wondering which of the dignitaries would be the first to slip on a bead and fall flat on his backside. On the marble floor the beads were rolling back and forth like ball bearings and I had already seen a waiter come perilously close to sloshing a tray of canapés over the Commercial Minister. Several people came up and said, 'I saw you on television. You're the lady whose little horses are too big.'

Luckily there was no casualties that night and Edgardo and the Chargé d'Affaires promised to do everything in their power to see that Sr Goldmann fulfilled his contract.

Even though Argentina and Chico were not the horses I

had ordered, it was impossible not to grow very attached to them. They were very affectionate and docile and we never had the slightest trouble with them as we traipsed around the country, visiting television studios and the Motor Show at Earls Court where they were put on a display – appropriately enough – at the Deux Chevaux stand. They proved to be a child's dream animals, not just because they were small and gentle but because they never seemed to mind how many small people flocked around to pet them, and never kicked or bit.

Correspondence with Sr Goldmann in the meantime seemed to be getting me nowhere. I had no idea when (or if) the second pair of horses I had paid for would be sent. Sr Goldmann had made vague excuses about how we would have to wait until the spotted horses bred again since there were none available for sale at that moment. The only solution, clearly, was to go to Argentina and confront Sr Goldmann in person.

14

The First Falabellas

You can keep your morale up for just so long by pretending that everything will work out for the best because your heart is in it, even if all the figures are against you. But sooner or later, over a bank statement or a monthly account lying among the debris of the breakfast table, you have to face up to hard facts.

The fifth year of the wildlife park was the most testing. We knew it was going to be the make-or-break year. As the bills piled up and the long winter drew to a close, we kept asking ourselves whether, this year, we could reach that magic figure of 100,000 visitors that we hoped would enable us to keep the zoo going.

The animals seemed to share our gloom that winter. It is not just the humans at Kilverstone who tend to get a bit grumpy and dispirited when the cold settles in and the visitors curl up at home in front of their heaters and television sets. I walked down one chilly morning with Nickit wrapped up in his blanket to talk to the otters, Slip and Slide. They were the most gregarious show-offs in the whole park and they were miserable without an audience. During the season they were never happier than when they had attracted a crowd, giving vent freely to its 'oohs' and 'ahs'. They had a very professional way of rising on their hind legs and taking their bows, just like cabaret performers. That winter morning I found them swaying about on their hind legs, impatient to start the show. They looked as if they were saying, 'Roll up, roll up, the curtain's going up!'

At first they seemed glad to see me and showed off their backstroke in the pool. Slip did a couple of underwater somersaults. But then, tired of playing to an almost deserted house, they threw a sulk worthy of a prima donna and retired into their little house.

'Never mind,' I whispered to them through the glass, 'you'll have an audience before long. This year we're going to make it. We have to.'

That year we became the perfect circus family. We hired a public relations firm to help to promote the park and before long their work started to show results. John and I would be off at short notice to appear on television programmes up and down the country and each new appearance brought a flood of new visitors, many of them from far afield.

We took bandit the raccoon as well as Pinchit and Nickit, the baby capuchin monkeys, down to Bristol with us for an appearance on the 'Animal Magic' programme. Nickit, being very small and timid, clung tightly to me and wouldn't be budged. Pinchit, now an adventurous teenager (in monkey terms), was keen to make the most of the show and hopped on to the shoulder of Johnny Morris, the presenter, to whom he chatted away happily. We had a little bit of trouble with Bandit, who was not very happy about being exiled to the upper branches of a tree in the studio, where the cameramen wanted to film him. Every time he was coaxed up there he would soon slide down again. Finally John hit upon the idea of spiking the branches with pieces of fruit – chunks of apple, banana and pear – as an incentive to Bandit to stay. This worked perfectly and Bandit had a highly successful début as a television star.

We trooped around wherever people wanted to interview us and wherever we thought we could get a good crowd interested in the park. We paraded for four and a half miles along the Yarmouth seafront with a collection of Kilverstone creatures during a carnival there. It was an exhausting day, with Charles in particular being the butt for the inevitable jokes from the crowd about the number of monkeys at Kilverstone. But the day had its funny moments. Halfway through the parade, one of the little horses peed copiously in the middle of the street, producing an enormous puddle. This seemed to appeal tremendously to the crowd.

'How can that little thing hold all that water?' someone yelled.

'Same again, please,' piped up another spectator.

We slaved away from dawn till dusk re-doing the entrance to the park, putting up flagpoles and bunting, setting up a patting area where the children could come to close quarters with rabbits and goats and baby lambs and expanding our adventure playground to include a Wild West stockade. But the elements were against us. It snowed through Easter and we shivered indoors, like most of the people who would otherwise have come to the park. Most people also stayed away during the Jubilee bank holiday, attending their own neighbourhood celebrations.

Yet, if the summer was cruel, the winter was quite kind. There was a mellow sun through most of the winter months which helped to keep most of the animals going. And when it came to totting up the figures for the whole year, we found that the number of visitors had risen to that magic number – 100,000. Ceremonially John uncorked a bottle of champagne and handed me my glass.

'Wait,' I said. 'The animals did it as much as us. Let's share it with them.'

Solemnly we trooped down to the spider monkeys' cage and as Eric gave me a hug I offered him my glass. He stuck a finger in it, tasted it, but obviously the vintage was not to his liking as he grimaced, shook his head and climbed up to the roof of his cage.

With the first year of 100,000 visitors under our belts, only one cloud remained on the horizon: the money which we felt we had paid to Sr Goldmann under false pretences. We had planned a return visit to Peru early in the New Year, five months or so after Argentina and Chico arrived at Kilverstone. It seemed easy and agreeable enough to add Argentina to our itinerary to see if we could meet Sr Goldmann and bring back the twenty-inch horses he had originally promised.

We left England on a miserable January day when a heavy snowfall had dissolved into grey, nasty slush. We were happy to be heading south to the sun. Fifteen hours later we were flying over the vast sprawl of Buenos Aires, an enormous, muscular city whose squares and parks and ritzy shops – especially around the endless pedestrian shopping mall, Florida – rival those of Rome or Madrid. We stayed at the Plaza Hotel, a charming, Parisian establishment, temptingly close to the smart shops of Florida. Our only complaint was about the pavements, which were lethal to the unwary pedestrian since half the paving stones were uneven or missing altogether.

We were taken in hand by family friends who showed us the sights of the town and we gorged ourselves shamelessly on Argentine steaks, which are undoubtedly the best in the world. It is the Argentinians not the Americans (and certainly not the down-at-heel British) who are the world's champion beef-eaters. It is not unknown for gauchos to consume several pounds of meat at a single sitting. An Argentine barbecue, or asado, is not soon forgotten.

Alec Shaw of the Banco Shaw was one of the first people to contact us. He took us to the Jockey Club for dinner, where we learned that his great hobby was naval and military history and that he was a tremendous admirer of John's grandfather. Alec introduced us to Carlos Mehano-vich, a leading Argentine conservationist, who pressed us to spend a weekend at his ranch. Since we still did not know when our showdown with Sr Goldmann would take place we gratefully accepted.

We went by train to the ranch, which was about 300 miles outside the capital. For most of the journey we saw flocks of birds, especially screamers. The ranch was called La Cautiva ('The Captive'), a reminder of a bloody past summed up by an old painting that Carlos kept in the main living-room, showing an Indian raiding party carrying off a white woman from the ranch. The house was beautiful: long and low and white, with pillars and a shady verandah and, to our delight, a flock of rheas strolling about the lawn. We would walk to the main house for dinner at night from the pink guest house where we slept by the light of the fireflies flitting about the garden.

Carlos drove us over endless rolling pampas. Wherever there was a dip in the land natural ponds had been formed by the rains and these were a haven for many birds. In Argentina rheas are often killed for their feathers and the skins are used for bags and other leather goods. Carlos had taken it upon himself to provide a natural reserve for the birds on his property. From time to time he would have the particularly valuable feathers plucked from the younger rheas in order to protect them from being killed by poachers for their feathers.

On our return from the ranch another Argentine friend got hold of Sr Goldmann and summoned him to meet us at the Plaza late one morning. An extraordinary figure turned up: huge, shambling, with a bulbous paunch that his trousers seemed barely able to contain and a great, jutting nose. He looked rather like Fagin in the old film of *Oliver Twist*. He professed not to understand English so our friend was cast in the rôle of interpreter. In effect he did our bargaining for us, which was a great relief since Sr Goldmann was an incredibly slippery customer.

'Look, everyone is very angry about what you've done,' our friend explained. 'Apart from the upset to my friends, you've brought a lot of bad publicity for Argentina and the people in the Ministry of Economy are so furious that I think there's a good chance that your export licence will be revoked unless you make amends.'

'Are you threatening me?' Goldmann blustered, rising up menacingly from his chair and shaking a meaty fist in the air.

'It's not a question of threats,' our friend riposted. 'It's just that you've cheated my friends and for once you're not going to get away with it.'

At this Sr Goldmann assumed the most ingratiating, self-pitying expression, wringing his hands and appealing to us in a whining voice. 'Please, please understand, Excelencias,' he said, 'it is I, Juan Goldmann, who has been cheated. I gave the money to my business partner who breeds the horses. I have no money to give you, since he has it.'

The conversation rapidly fell after this, with Sr Goldmann contradicting himself every few minutes. At one point he waved a letter of credit for £100,000, presumably to convince us that he was good for the money. It was finally agreed that he owed us $12,800 – the price of the horses that had not been delivered, plus partial restitution of the price of the horses we had already been sent. But Sr Goldmann said he would prefer to pay us by letting us have three horses instead of the two we were still owed. He promised to take us out to his partner's ranch where, he said, we would be able to choose any three horses that took our fancy.

He finally shuffled off, all smiles and reassurances, and we settled in to recover at the luxurious bar of the Plaza.

'Whew, I'm glad that's cleared up at last,' said John.

But it wasn't. We now had to endure endless telephoning back and forth as Sr Goldmann hit upon one excuse after another for not taking us to his partner's ranch. The plot thickened on a Thursday that we spent exploring the La Plata Zoo. On our return to the hotel there was an urgent message from a Mr Beaton, the Commercial Counsellor at the British Embassy. When we rang back he told us that Goldmann's partner had a police record and that it was thought unwise for us to get involved in any business dealings with that lot. He also told us that Sr Falabella, the current head of the family that had given its name to the little horses, was most concerned about what had happened and was anxious to talk to us, if possible over dinner that night.

So we went round to meet Mr Beaton and found that Sr Falabella and his lawyer, a descendant of the famous Argentine General Roca, were already there. Sr Falabella was a tall, stately man in an immaculate deep-blue suit, seventy years old but looking ten years younger. He quickly put us in the picture.

'That good-for-nothing, Sr X, has been stealing my horses,' he declared. 'I've been planning to take legal action myself. You can work out the whole thing if you just take a look at this.'

With the aid of Mr Beaton we were able to decipher the first few lines which were indeed enough to explain everything. According to the file, Sr Goldmann's partner had already been charged with three serious offences – twice for attempted rape and once for rape and inflicting grievous bodily harm. He was also believed to be a confidence trickster and a drug pusher. He sounded a real charmer.

'So you can see that you aren't the first ones this scoundrel has deceived,' Sr Falabella concluded. 'In fact, since I heard about your case I have found out that some people in France have been sent even bigger horses than yours, even though they were promised, like you, horses less than twenty inches tall.'

The best confidence trick of all had apparently involved no less a personage than the King of Spain. Sr X had gone to the Spanish Embassy and said that he wanted to present some miniature horses to the King of Spain. Delighted by the gesture, the Spanish government took care of his expenses on a trip to Madrid. He turned up without the horses but had a wonderful time carousing around the town. The King never got his little horses.

Sr Falabella was anxious to put an end to the whole business because it was doing damage to the reputation of his miniature horses and the good name of Argentina. He invited us out to his ranch to look at his herds. We were taken to one field where more than 400 little horses were rounded up for us. There were all colours – skewbald, piebald, black, brown, palomino, creamy horses and spotted ones. Most of them were larger than we wanted, up to three feet high. But in another field Sr Falabella's gauchos mustered twenty or so really tiny horses.

The dominant figure in the second field was a tiny, perfectly formed black stallion who was very busy rounding up his mares and herding them away from the gaucho's big horse. He would rear up in front of the big horse and then wheel about with his hind legs flashing out behind.

'Now,' said Sr Falabella, 'I will take you to see the spotted stallion in your photograph.' Down the great driveway, flanked by phalanxes of eucalyptus trees, he led us to yet another field. And there was Menelec, the horse from the photograph.

'That,' said Sr Falabella, 'is my best horse. He has fathered all the spotted horses that you have seen on the ranch.'

'He's the one I want,' I said instantly. 'I simply must have him.'

'Well, after everything you have had to put up with, it would be a pity to send you home disappointed.'

We spent the rest of the day choosing two other stallions and three mares to take back with Menelec. Prize Falabellas, alas, do not come cheap.

Over lunch with Sr Falabella I said, 'I've heard so many stories, each more far-fetched than the last, about how your little horses came to be this size. Will you tell me the true story?'

'Gladly,' he replied. 'Certain of the Indian tribes who inhabited parts of Chile and Argentina were so fierce and war-like that even the Spaniards could not subdue them or conquer them. They were nomadic tribes and would descend on the ranches in Argentina in the early days, kill all the men, women and children and drive off the cattle. When they had many thousands of head of cattle they would drive them over the mountains into Chile and sell them there. The only ones they spared in their murderous raids were the young and pretty women, whom they would carry off. Often they would cut the skin off the palms of their captives' hands and the soles of their feet, or cut the tendons of their legs so that they could not run away or even crawl away.

'They were very brave, those early settlers in Argentina, always living under constant fear of Indian attack. My own maternal grandfather was an Irishman called Newton who had a great love and a great knowledge of horses. There was nothing he didn't know about them, either about curing their ills or about breeding and training them.

'There was a river on my grandfather's ranch and here he built his house and a mill. Every night he placed stones in the mill-wheel and the rumbling noise they made could be heard miles away. The Indians thought he must be a magician and on the whole gave him a fairly wide berth.

'As my grandfather had the only water for some miles around, and there was a ford below his house, often horses came to the river to drink. Sometimes four horses would appear pulling a carriage with no one in it, only blood on the seats, or a horse saddled and bridled with no rider but blood on the saddle: the owners had been ambushed and murdered by the Indians.

'Then one day there came to his river to drink a horse that he saw with his experienced eye was very different. He could see it had dwarf sickness' – this is the nearest equivalent to the untranslatable Spanish word our host used – 'and that it would breed very small horses. So from this one horse he bred very small, perfectly proportioned little horses for his small daughter who became my mother.'

But of course no one knows how that horse came to be the size it was. What was its breeding? Where had it come from? No one knew; its owners were dead. Eohippus, the first horse, was tiny, only the size of a dog, and originated in North America. Some of its descendants went north and across the land bridge which is now the Bering Strait into Asia and then Europe. All horses evolved from these. Some of the original little horses went south into South America, but it is believed that all these horses died out, in both North and South America. Wouldn't it be nice to think that some of those tiny horses had survived, say in some lost valley, and that this was their descendant?

Now I was letting my imagination run away with me. Still, the real story Sr Falabella had told me was just as romantic as any I had heard or could make up. He went on to explain about the Falabella horses.

'You will find the mares are very keen to mate but the stallions are much slower. They seem to think they have to pay for it, and only when they realise they don't have to pay do they get keen.' He added that you could give them a little cocaine to get rid of their inhibitions and make them mate sooner.

I thought I had got the word wrong from the Spanish but no, he repeated, 'Just a little cocaine, it will help them a lot.'

I had terrible thoughts of trying to explain to the local police why I had cocaine in my possession: 'Just to make my stallions randy.' Who would believe me? Visions of headlines in the *News of the World* flashed before my eyes.

'No, thank you,' I said firmly. 'I'll wait till they feel like it.'

We were very happy about our new horses and made arrangements for them to be flown to England within days of our own departure. This time we were taking no risks. Back in Buenos Aires, however, we had to endure another maddening round of lies and broken promises from Sr

Goldmann, who clearly had no intention of giving us what he owed us if he could possibly sidle out of it. We spent a whole day at the hotel waiting for him to come and fetch us to see the horses he had told us about, in order to choose three to take home with us. After many phone calls back and forth he finally slouched in at about 5.30 p.m. with his shopping under his arm to tell us in an off-handed way that there was no chance of going that day.

Our Argentine friends, whose tempers must have been even more badly frayed than ours by this stage, rallied round once more and we were taken along to see some officials at the Ministry of Finance. They were very sympathetic but said that all they could do was to revoke Goldmann's export licence as a punishment for his dishonest dealings with us and other buyers. In fact this did happen. The rest would be up to us and our lawyers if we wanted to go ahead and sue.

I was a little nervous about the thought of legal action, especially since it would be brought in our absence in a foreign court in a far-off country. I was rather prejudiced, since my step-grandfather, who had been a QC and a High Court Judge, had once advised me never to go to court if I could possibly help it. 'That only helps the lawyers who make money out of you,' he used to say. Of course, this argument did not go down very well with the Argentine lawyers who were advising us! But we ended by leaving the whole affair in the competent hands of Julio Falabella's lawyer. Perhaps it was only a shot in the dark but you've got to try. He was still pursuing the case when these words were written.

The Falabellas became the most popular residents at Kilverstone. The first question most people ask when they arrive at the wildlife park is, 'Where are the little horses?'

The Falabellas were equally popular with the research scientists at the equine research centre at Newmarket. 'This is the first time,' one of them told John, 'that we have been able to get an entire horse on our X-ray screen. You can't get a clear picture with an ordinary horse; the X-ray shows a large grey splodge with only backbone and ribs showing. This is the pancreas and here are the kidneys and here the liver. We've never seen them on X-ray before.'

And our mating games went on to the wonderment – and occasional embarrassment – of our visitors. Come the season in late spring, the first question our children would ask, coming up to Kilverstone for the weekend, would be, 'Are you mating again?'

15

Adventures of a Norfolk Vet

Gerald Durrell warns in one of his books that you should never let a vet or an architect near a zoo. After our teething troubles with the park we were inclined to agree with him about architects: the quickest, simplest and most economical way to get a new animal house or aviary set up seemed to be to design and build it ourselves. John, the butler, turned out to be a first-rate bricklayer and carpenter and he was soon to be seen more often hammering nails into a roof than about the house.

Anyone who keeps animals is also obliged to get to know the symptoms of his charges' possible complaints but there is really no such thing as a do-it-yourself vet unless you are prepared to go the whole hog and do the medical training. We were lucky to have a good-natured, highly dedicated local vet called Bill Marriott. Bill soon became a familiar figure at Kilverstone, a tweedy figure rolling up in his Toyota, its back seat crammed with bottles and veterinary kit. Sometimes he would bring his son along too to look round the park.

Bill Marriott's patients at Kilverstone were a world removed from his usual clients – sheep and cows and dogs and cats. Finding himself confronted with strange creatures from the tropics with unpronounceable names, he somehow managed to stay quite unflappable. I suppose that in a way his predicament was only a dramatised version of what most vets have to contend with in their professional lives. After all, a doctor has only one species to treat whereas a vet has to get the hang of all sorts of species that walk or jump or fly.

We called on Mr Marriott for the first time one Saturday afternoon in the summer before the park was officially opened. We had been moving in our first animal guests and one or two of them were having a bit of trouble in adjusting to the switch in climate and scenery. John called Mr Marriott to announce, 'We've got a coatimundi with a runny tummy.'

'Say again, please,' Mr Marriott came back in obvious disbelief. 'A coati *what*?'

John firmly repeated the beast's name.

'Hm. I see. Well, I'll be round as quick as I can,' Mr Marriott said matter-of-factly, as if coatimundis turned up in Thetford every other day.

The coati is in fact a South American cousin of the panda bear, like the raccoon and the kinkajou. Coatis have long, ringed tails, which they often carry along waving high above their backs, and a very long, sensitive nose with which they snuffle around for insects and worms in the ground. We bought a female coati, our first animal for the park, because we saw her in a pet shop in Essex in a cage so small that she could hardly turn round.

'It's ghastly,' I said to John. 'We must buy her and get her out of here.'

As we drove back to Kilverstone with our first coati snuffling about on the back seat in a makeshift cage, we decided to call her Sniffles and when we found a mate for her he would be Snuffles. In those early days before we had any keepers I looked after any birds or animals we acquired. Sniffles was so keen on her food that she seemed to think that the hand that fed her could well be the hand that took it away, and one day she gave my finger a rather nasty bite. The coati's habit of exploring every promising mound of earth for a snack meant that she had revoltingly dirty teeth, and not only my hand but my whole arm blew up like a balloon.

I don't know whether Mr Marriott had had time to consult his library but he betrayed no sign that he was in the least surprised to encounter his new patient. He did, however, press his finger to his nose.

'Phew,' he exclaimed. 'It's not a pretty sight, is it?'

It was not. Although in Latin America diarrhoea is often referred to as 'Montezuma's revenge', Snuffles must have been feeling that something in the English air, or the English worms, had been specially calculated to do her in. The mess was all over the walls of her pen.

Mr Marriott eyed Sniffles and Sniffles eyed him back. With the pale patches around her eyes, she looked rather like an old woman peering through big round spectacles.

'Charles,' I called to my younger son, 'we don't want Mr Marriott to get bitten by Sniffles on his first day at Kilverstone. You'd better come and hold her down.'

Charles took it with relatively good grace. 'I hope you've got something like that for me if Sniffles does get her teeth into me,' he observed to Mr Marriott as the vet checked his syringe.

Sniffles wriggled and squirmed while Charles wrestled to hold her steady. Mr Marriott peered and probed and finally jabbed in the needle.

'That's fine. Now, just get her teeth open for me,' he said to Charles. Tentatively, Charles slipped his fingers into Sniffles' mouth. 'Take it easy, there are good things coming,' said the vet.

The coati must have understood him, since she was surprisingly well-behaved. Mr Marriott slipped her a children's brand of syrup, laced with antibiotics.

'That should do the trick,' he said as he gingerly extricated himself from the pen. 'What I would suggest,' he went on as he strolled over to the house with us for tea, 'is that it would be a good idea if you would keep me posted on what new animals you're bringing to the park. That way, I can mug up on them before you have to call me in – you know, keep one foot ahead of the field.'

It was not long before we discovered that Mr Marriott was traipsing around the country, dropping in at meetings of zoo vets and becoming quite a wildlife expert. Most of his adventures at Kilverstone revolved around how to catch and grab hold of some unwilling beast or bird in order to give it its medicine. I asked Mr Marriott to record some of his own recollections of how things developed after that first visit to the park:

'I had to spend a good deal of time working out how to get injections into different animals. In the case of the bigger birds, like the flamingos and the crowned cranes, pinioning takes quite a bit of practice and it's not at all like tying down a farmyard duck. I only really mastered the technique by comparing notes with people who have experienced the same problems – with the staff at Whipsnade Zoo, for example.

'Spider monkeys are easy enough to inject provided you can catch them. The first time I tried was in the early days of the park. One of the female monkeys had been taken ill and I needed to give her a shot in a hurry. The keepers came after her with a catching net that had been hastily prepared. As soon as she looked to be safely inside it, however, she managed to find a hole where no hole seemed to exist. I had examined her as well as I could and had just got ready to give her a jab into whatever appendage I could grab hold of – I think it was her hind leg – when one of her hands shot out from nowhere and snatched the syringe away from me. Arms and legs seemed to be shooting out in all directions and there was my syringe, waving about like a wand in mid-air.

'We could only catch some of the bigger animals in order to examine and treat them with the aid of a dart gun. I used to get regular target practice on a Sika deer, happily known as Naughty Seeker, who would get more and more irritable and aggressive every autumn as the mating season drew on. Normally quite gentle and shy, this buck would become viciously aggressive towards any human and any other male that approached him. Either he would have to be penned up in a separate enclosure of his own, or we would have to get hold of him and prune his antlers. The only way I could get near him to remove his antlers was to anaesthetise him with a shot from the dart gun.

'One of the main differences between the life of an ordinary vet and that of someone who has to treat wild animals is that it is rarely possible to sit down and take a calm look at the patient if you are dealing with un-domesticated species. You often have to begin by deciding whether you can work out what is wrong with an animal from afar or whether you will have to catch it in order to take a closer look. I spent the best part of an afternoon hunting down one of Naughty Seeker's lady friends to have a look at a nasty lump that had suddenly appeared on her behind. It took a long time because every time we managed to approach within range of the dart gun she would flash away to the other side of the paddock. I realised that I was not quite up to SAS marksmanship standards when we had a go at ambushing her. In the first two shots, all I managed to do was to immobilise two trees. It took another half-hour's stalking before I finally managed to get a dart into her backside.

'At Kilverstone, of course, wild animals lead a sheltered life. They are not going to wind up as a snack for their natural predators. They receive instant veterinary attention if they fall sick. They may face one or two hazards that you won't find in the jungle, as a result of thoughtless behaviour by the public. For instance, Lord Fisher once showed me some anti-depressant pills that had been found inside a raccoon pen. Maybe they dropped out of a lady's handbag. At least, that's what one likes to think.

'But the point is that the animals at Kilverstone have a far better chance of living to a ripe old age than they would ever enjoy in the wild. And of course they are better off than farmyard animals too, since a farmer will cull his herds as their economic efficiency falls. A farmyard animal is really like an element in a meat factory that will be dispensed with when it becomes profitable to do so or unprofitable to do otherwise. The animals who have the best chance of achieving old age, apart from domestic pets, are animals in wildlife parks.

'Time and again at Kilverstone I have been forcibly struck by the amazing ability of nature to heal in its own mysterious ways, sometimes in situations where medicine could offer no further help. The way the rhea whose head had nearly been bitten off by a maned wolf recovered was little short of miraculous. We had done what we could, but it was nature that finished the job.

'I remember a similar case involving a Sika deer that skeltered into a fence after some visitor had ignored the signs and left the gate to the deer park open so that the animals could stray out. The doe badly gashed her lips and broke her jaw while trying to get back into the deer park. We did not realise how bad the injuries were until we put her under sedation. Then I saw that her whole lower lip had been torn off from the gum and was dangling down like a bit of orange peel still hanging by a sliver. The jawbone was badly fractured on the left-hand side.

'Her case looked pretty hopeless, but I tried to patch her up as best I could, moved by the gentle beauty of this kind of deer. Rather to my surprise she made an astonishing recovery. Within a few months her mouth had largely mended and she was able to feed normally again. The only odd sign was that she kept her winter coat, right into midsummer.

'The monkeys, of course, are the most fascinating creatures in the park to most people, including my son, because of their extraordinary range of expression and behaviour – and above all because they resemble us, sometimes more closely than we might care to think. Some of the resemblances have medical importance. You have to keep this in mind during the quarantine stage, when new monkeys have just arrived, since the viral diseases that they may have picked up may well be infectious to human attendants. But throughout the life of the monkeys one is repeatedly reminded of the human connection. So many of their health problems resemble ours – respiratory ailments, colds and so on. I was able to draw on specialist medical knowledge of rare human ailments in my efforts to treat the spider monkeys. I sent off X-rays of signs of wasting in the left leg of one of the younger monkeys to a leading children's orthopaedic surgeon, whose advice was of considerable value. Sadly, the monkey turned out to have a form of spina bifida and there was nothing we could do in the end to save her.'

Mr Marriott's favourite animal, we soon discovered, was the tapir. I suspect that this may have been because our tapirs don't kick and fight so much about having to see the doctor as other wild animals tend to do. Our tapirs just love to be petted and tickled. They took a great liking to Mr Marriott and would roll over on their backs in apparent ecstasies after he started scratching them behind the ears. Still, even the friendly tapir can tell the difference between a hand that comes to tickle and one that comes bearing down on it with a hypodermic needle, and it reacts.

The day came when Bill Marriott had to give our tapir, Marcus, a penicillin injection. Marcus obviously felt betrayed when his friend the vet, after making him roll around in delight by tickling him, suddenly seized his chance to plunge in the needle. Marcus turned a baleful eye on Mr Marriott and Brian Dickson, who had helped to hold him steady. A tapir may not look like a very combative beast on an average day, but there is a lot of meat on its bones and at that moment Marcus was putting on his very best imitation of an enraged wild boar about to charge.

'My God!' said Brian, 'I think he's going to go for us.'

Sure enough, inside the tapir house, Marcus was beginning to stalk Brian and the vet like a hunting dog. The two men hastily made for safety on the other side of the paddock wall while Marcus, who had begun to sound like an irate steam engine, quickened his pace behind.

'Quick, quick. Over the wall,' Brian gasped.

Mr Marriott made it just in time but in his haste to haul himself over the wall, which is about four and a half feet high, he caused Brian to lose his footing.

'Yeeowtch!' shouted Brian.

Marcus had left him with two fine gashes in the back of his trousers, big enough for a tapir to put its head through. None of us like injections but our animals have their own way of making their feelings known.

16

The Falabellas
Meet the Queen

The following year, our sixth, we had our first spider monkey babies. There were two pregnant mothers, Pamela and Cleo, competing to produce. Cleo made it first and gave birth to a girl who looked exactly like Mr Gandhi although my children thought it looked more like Kojak – spider monkey babies are totally bald at birth. We called the girl Carmen, after the sister of our friend Felipe Benavides, who had looked after the parents in Peru before they were sent across. We were rather worried about Carmen at first. The mother seemed to keep her nipples under her arm and there was no show of milk at the beginning so we began to wonder whether Carmen was getting anything to drink but everything turned out to be all right and she began to feed satisfactorily.

Pamela, the other mother-to-be, became very broody while waiting to give birth to her own offspring. She would constantly grab Cleo's baby off her back and cuddle it for a while. Cleo, being a rather timid little creature, would not snatch it back but would have to wait until Pamela released it and it would slowly crawl back to her. This tug-of-love game was not good for poor little Carmen. The keepers rushed up to me with her one day and she looked dreadful. I think that her rib-cage must have been damaged during one of Pamela's grabs at her. She looked cold and utterly miserable. We put her in front of a radiator in an effort to warm her up and I managed to feed her some milk in a bottle. But we had got to her too late and she died in the course of the night.

Pamela gave birth to her own baby not long after but the exertion of the labour must have been too much for her. During the birth Pamela suffered a haemorrhage in an artery leading to the heart. Nothing could be done to save her. We were abroad the night the baby was born and we heard afterwards that the poor little mite must have spent the night going from one female to another. It ended up wrapped round the neck of Eric, the father. The keepers did not find it until the next morning. There was a sense of tragedy in the spider monkeys' cage when they came to inspect. All the other monkeys became extremely distressed when the keepers approached the baby. Carefully they removed Pamela's body. The problem then was to get hold of her baby in order to feed it. Eric was clinging to it with all his might.

They had to give Eric tranquillisers before they could get the baby away from him. But even that didn't work. After one pill he was as determined as before. After a second he started jumping up and down, yelling blue murder. Since no one was quite sure how many tranquillisers a spider monkey could take without ill effects, the keepers decided at that point to go in with a catching net. They put it on the ground while they tried to work out the best way to snare him without starting a panic. Obligingly, Eric decided to solve the problem for them. He picked up the net and draped it over his head and shoulders as if it were a fancy-dress costume. All the keepers had to do was to reach up inside the net and disentangle the clinging baby.

Stuart, the monkey keeper, and his girl friend – who

luckily for us was a nurse – brought up the baby for several days before we came home. I was sad to hear of Pamela's death but delighted to have a new baby in the house. It was the first spider monkey we had tried to rear inside Kilverstone Hall. The television series, 'Starsky and Hutch', was all the rage at the time and I thought that the new baby looked exactly like the character Huggy Bear in the series. So that is what we called him.

From the first, Huggy Bear seemed destined for an adventurous social life. Not long after he was brought into the house, we took him to a restaurant in the district which was as starchy as only country restaurants can be. The owner is a marvellous chef but a holy terror to guests who do not meet his own rigorous standards. He had been known to greet customers who arrive late with a tray laden with the food that they were intended to eat – and to throw it at them.

So we were a little nervous about arriving with a spider monkey in tow. I disguised Huggy's basket as best I could by tying a chiffon scarf round it; it still looked rather strange to be going out on the town in evening dress with a square basket over my arm. The proprietor sailed into the room and started chatting away to the people at the next table. I heard them telling him that they had acquired a new dog.

'It's a bloody good thing you didn't bring it with you,' he glared.

I quaked, and leaned down to make sure that Huggy Bear was securely hidden. I was alarmed because Huggy seemed to be pulling the scarf in across his face and I thought that if he went on pulling he was liable to suffocate himself. I started trying to adjust the scarf, my steak au poivre forgotten on the table. Seeing my contortions under the tablecloth, the proprietor rushed over in our direction, apparently thinking I had dropped my napkin on the floor.

'Madame, madame, allow me,' he gushed.

'Oh no,' I exclaimed, pulling the tablecloth over my knees

and sending a wine glass flying. 'Please let us enjoy your excellent food.'

The proprietor looked reprovingly at the pink pool that was extending itself over his Irish linen, set his nose at a commanding angle and strode away.

'Another near escape,' sighed John.

Leading a social life with a baby monkey on your lap is no joke.

A few days later we drove down to Ugbrooke for the twenty-first birthday party of my niece, Sarah. Huggy, of course, had to come too. They had set up a discothèque for the dance and Huggy joined in the jiving and sampled the Buck's Fizz. I think he must have found the beat a bit fast because he soon became very clingy and we put him to bed upstairs.

My sister-in-law, Kay, very kindly used to put silk sheets on the four-poster when we came to stay. They were, indeed, the same sheets that had been used by King George V and Queen Mary, and there were fortunately quite a few pairs since they had had to be changed for royalty every day. It always gave me a burst of nostalgia to see those silk sheets, because when my sister Mary and I were children, our nanny used to cut up the sheets to make us petticoats and knickers. We used to call them 'the King's sheets', and I remember that one day I came bursting into the sitting-room at Ugbrooke after scrambling up a tree, pulled up my skirt to display my torn knickers, not knowing there were guests, and shouted, 'Look, I've torn the King's sheets again.'

By this stage there was only one pair of the original silk sheets left, no doubt as a result of nanny's scissors and my tomboy depredations. So we always felt rather flattered when Kay got them out. We slept in the Cardinal's Room, which is very grandly done up in Cardinal reds and presided over by the portrait of a Clifford ancestor who was a prince of the Church. He seemed to be looking down at me very disapprovingly over his beaky nose as I climbed into the bed with Huggy. At the foot of the bed is a great chest full of the Cardinal's regalia, which Hugh liked to dress up in as a child when no adults were looking.

Huggy loved the silk sheets and there was really no way of keeping him off them. He was a very demanding baby and had to be fed every two hours during the night. All the other jungle babies I had reared, monkeys, jaguars, raccoons or badgers had slept in a little basket by my bed if ever we had taken them to other people's houses. But not Huggy. Bodily contact is so important to spider monkeys that they often sleep in heaps, all touching each other. At Ugbrooke Huggy seemed determined to howl all night and none of us got any sleep. In desperation I took him into the bed and soon found that he would only sleep in the crook of my arm where he could hear my heart beat. He and John slept well after that but my sleep was very fitful as I was worried about squashing him. John had got used by now to monkey stuff in bed but I think that Hugh and Kay found it a bit odd that he even had to compete with a baby monkey for a place between the silk sheets.

The morning after the party we took Huggy on an expedition with us to Paignton Zoo. On our return we found reporters and cameramen all over Ugbrooke. Someone had told the press that a baby spider monkey was sleeping in the four-poster bed that King George V and Queen Mary had occupied during their stay at Ugbrooke.

'Things ain't what they used to be,' Hugh harrumphed, twitching his side-whiskers.

'Have they come to photograph me?' asked Sarah hopefully, blinking in the light. 'Ouch! You'd better tell them to wait until I do my hair.'

'They're only interested in Latin American monkeys,' said Hugh. 'And by the way, what time did you get to bed last night, my girl?'

'Huggy, we're going to make you a star,' said the man from the Exeter newspaper. And they did.

'I'm not getting undressed at this time of day,' I said firmly, so I got into bed fully dressed between the silk sheets, with Huggy snuggled down beside me. Just our faces and chins could be seen against the down-filled pillows.

The next morning we found that Huggy's choice of resting-place had turned him into an instant celebrity. His face seemed to be in every newspaper and the story was carried as far afield as Australia. Television was just as keen as the newspapers. By the time he was three weeks old, Huggy had made six television appearances.

'It's going to be like living with Shirley Temple,' John groaned after we had visited yet another television studio.

Of course, publicity was what we wanted and needed in order to bring people to Kilverstone and secure the future of the park we had worked so hard to create, but after Huggy became famous life at Kilverstone was more than ever like living in a glasshouse.

The day after Huggy had made his press sensation we drove back to Kilverstone and I had just got the bags un-packed and had settled down to wash my hair when the telephone started ringing. First of all Thames Television rang me to ask whether I would go down to London that day so that Huggy could appear on the six o'clock news; they were prepared to send a taxi to fetch me. I thought I had better duck into Thetford to my local hairdresser and spruce myself up before going to London. When I got back I found that all hell had broken loose in the house.

'Quick, darling, you'd better get yourself sorted out,' said John. 'Two television crews are on their way and there are some press reporters here already. This is what stardom is all about.'

'Do you hear that, Huggy?' I said to the little black shape in my basket, now decked out in a woollen jumper and beanie that made him look even more like the character in 'Starsky and Hutch'. 'At this rate, you're going to be even more famous than your namesake.'

This lot of television people weren't going to settle for me in bed with Huggy fully dressed. 'What do you usually sleep in, Lady Fisher?' one of the producers asked.

I did not think it would be a good idea to show them one of my very flimsy nighties so I made for the bedroom and got into a dressing-gown.

'Now then, Lord Fisher, can we have you in the picture too, please?'

John hummed and hawed until I said to him, 'Hurry up, darling, or they'll think that we never sleep in the same bed.' He dashed off and re-emerged in his pyjamas. The cameras whirred.

Huggy seemed to be in constant demand. He started receiving fan mail from children all over the country. Some sent parcels containing sweets. One little girl even sent a love letter. Huggy was invited to appear on one television programme after another. I was particularly pleased when the 'Blue Peter' programme rang up and asked if we could bring Huggy round to the studios. When we got there we found that they had rigged up an enormous four-poster bed. Perhaps they thought that this was the only kind of furniture that made Huggy feel comfortable. I was a trifle nervous that day since it marked my thirteenth television appearance.

'Is that bed really going to hold together?' I asked uncertainly. 'It looks pretty wobbly to me.'

John gave it a push close to the bottom and it see-sawed back and forth.

'It's all right,' the studio manager insisted. 'We'll find something to prop up the base.'

We were delighted by the dressing-room, which was a real sign of Huggy's rise in show business status. We had been given a sumptuous room with vast mirrors, a chaise-longue and a private bathroom. On the door was a sign that read 'Lady Fisher and Huggy Bear'.

This time I kept my boots on in bed while the interviewer sat on the edge and Huggy listened in to the conversation, propped up against the pillows. John remarked to the interviewer afterwards, 'I don't let my wife go to bed with strangers unless she keeps her boots on.'

It became impossible to take Huggy anywhere without being recognised. And of course Huggy had to go everywhere with me because of his continual feeds and because I had to keep him warm: spider monkey babies are always attached to their mothers and need to have a constant feeling of nearness to them. Huggy would usually travel in his little basket with the chiffon scarf tied loosely over it. But as he grew bigger it became harder to keep him tucked away. A little black arm would slide out from under the scarf and start waving about.

One day I took Huggy shopping with me in Harrods. I was scouting around for some creams to save me from having my nose burned off on our next expedition to the Amazon. Hearing the girls' voices, Huggy became very excited. He is greatly attached to women and decided that this was the moment to make a grand entrée and hold court. I think he must also have been intrigued by the heady odours from the perfume counter. Suddenly he flung back the scarf and stood up in his basket, waving both arms, bobbing his head around in his little woollen beanie and chattering away in a cheeping voice, as if to say, 'It's me.'

The girl behind the counter clapped her hands and said, 'It must be Huggy Bear, it can't be anyone else.'

A crowd gathered quickly and I took a step backwards to give us some breathing space. Unhappily for us, someone had parked her poodle just behind me. Huggy and I went flying. My first thought was that I mustn't let Huggy crack his skull on the floor so I tried to hold his basket aloft with one hand while stretching out the other, laden with parcels, to break the fall. I found myself lying on the carpet on my chin, gasping for breath like a fish out of water.

As a result of these incidents Huggy began to develop a reputation for being a bit of a snob, sleeping between silk sheets, dining in the best restaurants and shopping at Harrods. But his fan mail grew and grew. One of the nicest letters he got came the next Christmas from a seven-year-old Thetford girl called Ellen Walker. Her letter read: 'Dear Huggy's Mummy and Little Huggy, My Mummy saw you in the Post Office. I was so sad not to have been with her as I love little Huggy very much and I hope that Huggy will play with the Teddy for Xmas. Love from Ellen Walker.'

With the letter, Ellen sent a little teddy bear and a tiny plastic gorilla. Huggy, of course, sent her a nice thank-you letter.

Huggy had acquired a very respectable wardrobe. My sister-in-law, Kay, had presented him with a fine set of knitted doll's clothes and we raided some of the old dolls' wardrobes tucked away in the storage rooms at Kilverstone. Huggy was quite the Little Lord Fauntleroy.

I had not known when I started rearing Huggy that spider monkeys are supposed to be one of the most difficult monkey species to rear successfully by hand. If I had understood how very delicate they are, I might have taken fright. Instead, I simply treated Huggy the way I would have treated any other monkey baby, and everything turned out for the best. Common sense will take you a very long way with monkey babies as with human babies. The similarities are enormous. A monkey baby, like any other, needs lots of cuddling and loving and comforting. One difference is that a monkey baby clings to its mother; the mother doesn't hold on to it – after all, her arms have to be free to climb and run and gather food. It's up to the baby to hold on; if it doesn't, it is liable to fall and be killed. During its first few months a spider monkey baby will hang on to its mother's tummy and then crawl around and cling to her back. Like human babies, monkey babies sleep most of the time. At the first sign of danger they will rush back to their mothers. As the monkey approaches the stage where it can move around independently, all the members of the troupe will play with it, helping to teach it by example, Discipline is pretty severe. A spider monkey baby may be allowed to get away with a few pranks like playing around with its mother's tail, but one step too far and it receives a formidable cuff.

When Huggy was brought into the house I found that he had a very upset tummy since he had been fed on Lactol, a processed milk that we use for raising cats. Monkeys need the same bottled milk as human babies. I gave Huggy SMA, which is the most digestible low-fat baby milk. Because of his indigestion I did what I had done with my own babies when they were very small: I would boil up some rice and use the strained water to make the feed.

While he stayed with us in the house Huggy acquired some very human pleasures. He enjoyed watching television more than any other monkey we had had in the house. It was only the monkeys, among our varied animal guests, who showed the slightest interest in television. It left Jubilee the baby jaguar, Bandit the raccoon and even Tia, our most domesticated chihuahua, totally indifferent. But the monkeys not only enjoyed television; in some cases they actually seemed to acquire new habits from it. I am convinced that Nickit started walking about on his knuckles as a result of watching the big apes on wildlife programmes.

Huggy Bear, for his part, became very much a ladies' man as he grew older, and would take special delight in television shows that had glamorous girls in them. Blondes were his great love. If some starlet bobbed up on the screen who particularly caught his eye, he would stick his lips through the bars of his cage, puckered up as if to give a big kiss.

Still, we had to reconcile ourselves to the thought that Huggy, like the other monkey babies before him, would finally have to go back to the monkey houses. I don't believe that monkeys can ever be fully domesticated or house trained, although some keepers have had more success in this respect than others. Marie Louise Benavides, our Peruvian friend, has kept all sorts of monkeys in her house, and she told me that she had once kept a titi monkey that she trained to go to the lavatory and to pull the chain when it had finished. I tried taking Nickit and Huggy to the loo but I was too frightened to let them experiment by themselves. They seemed so tiny, I was terrified that they might drown themselves through some mishap.

One morning when my children were staying at Kilverstone, Trina's small daughter, Pandora, let Huggy Bear out of his cage in the sitting-room. I found them happily sorting through that day's mail. I extracted a very grand-looking envelope from Huggy's fist and found that it was from the Queen's Equerry, Sir John Miller, who is in charge of the Royal coaches and horses. He was inviting us to bring the Falabellas to parade before the Queen on Smith's Lawn in Windsor Great Park between the finals of a polo match, when a number of other rare horses would also be put on display. Sir John also invited the Falabellas to stay overnight in the Royal Mews at Windsor Castle before their 'coming out'.

'How do you feel about becoming debutantes?' I asked the Falabellas in their paddock when I walked down after reading Sir John's letter.

Of course John and I were delighted and greatly honoured and had made up our minds to accept at once. But as I looked at the Falabellas, I realised that we had a problem. It was a sunny June day but they had all sprouted thick winter coats and looked a bit like horse-shaped teddy bears. It might have been summer in England but it was winter in Argentina and they had not adjusted to the change of home. In the hot weather their thick coats were obviously going to be too much for them. 'And you can't meet the Queen dressed like that,' I thought. So I had them clipped.

I dug out an enormous Victorian wicker pram that was tucked away in a store room and turned it into a miniature cart for Morenita, a winsome black Falabella, to pull. I had a white harness made for her, and thought it would be quite a sight to see her pulling Huggy Bear or Humphry – our newest black-and-white capuchin baby – along in their little cart. I was worried when the harness was not finished until the day before we were supposed to leave for Windsor, since Morenita had had no experience of pulling carriages and I thought she would need some practice if we were to avoid a small disaster in front of the Queen. Fortunately, Falabellas are very intelligent and surprisingly easy to train. Within a quarter of an hour or so Morenita was trotting along with the cart behind her as if she had been bred to do it.

We set off for Windsor with six little horses, plus Humphry the baby capuchin. (I thought that Huggy Bear had been getting quite enough public attention, and it was Humphry's turn to show off.) I annoyed John in the car on the way down by saying to him, 'You must scrub your hands very well before you see the Queen tomorrow. You know what the Queen Mother always says about the time she came to Kilverstone and met your father – that he had the dirtiest nails that she had ever seen!'

John's father was a very keen gardener who never cared about how he looked; presumably he had quite forgotten to scrub his nails before meeting the Queen. Looking at John's hands on the steering wheel – he had been digging in the walled gardens first thing that morning – I added, 'If you're not careful, the Queen is liable to think that you are carrying on the family tradition.'

'And if *you're* not careful, darling,' John came back, quick as a flash, 'she might think that you've married into the same tradition.'

I looked down and saw that my dress was covered with hair and muck from helping to load the crates containing the little horses and from cuddling Humphry all through the long drive.

When we arrived at the Royal Mews at Windsor we were directed to one of three magnificent courtyards, flanked with stables. Each of the stables was the size of a large family room with an equally large open space in front of it. The door posts were topped with large gilt balls with the letters ER II embossed on them. The mangers were so high that three of the Falabellas would have had to have stood one on top of the other to reach them. Inside the stables they looked quite lost, standing in soft deep straw up to their stomachs.

There was a great hustle and bustle after our arrival, with people coming up to take a peep at the Falabellas. Soon Sir John Miller arrived and helped us to get them settled in. We had given them their feed for the night and gone out into the courtyard when we saw the Queen driving herself down from the castle. She had given instruction to be informed as soon as the Falabellas arrived. Horses, of course, are a ruling passion among our Royal Family and the Queen is one of the most knowledgeable women in the world on the subject.

She came straight over to us and shook hands with John – dirty nails and all! I did my curtsy and automatically stretched out my right hand, forgetting for a moment that Oscar the ocelot had chewed off the tip of my index finger. I quickly remembered, and – deciding that I couldn't bear to have that finger squeezed in a handshake, even for the sake of the Queen of England – I stuck out my left hand instead, muttering something about a bite. The Queen got the surprise of being presented not only with my left hand but with a monkey's tail as well. Humphry had taken a firm grip on my left arm, with his long tail curled round the fingers of my left hand. Frightened by the novel surroundings, he was clinging on for dear life. The Queen did not bat an eyelid. She shook hands with Humphry's tail and my fingers and chatted on as if it was the most natural thing in the world.

The Queen was enchanted with the Falabellas and patted each one. She asked us how they came to be so small; she had heard the story of how the ancestors of the Falabellas had been trapped in a valley. I told her the real story, as Sr

Falabella had recounted it to us in Argentina. The Queen was worried that the little horses might do themselves some injury by eating their bedding, which they had started to sample in front of our eyes.

'Don't worry,' I reassured her. 'They're such little pigs that they'll try anything.'

After the Queen drove back to the castle, it struck me that in talking to her I had felt at once that I was speaking to a very old and close friend. She is remarkably kind and natural and has the great gift of being able to put people instantly at their ease. I've always been an ardent Royalist and every contact with our Royal Family has deepened my conviction that they are one of the greatest assets that Britain has.

The following day, dolled up and much cleaner, we paraded the horses round the polo field and lined them up in front of the Royal Box. The Queen, with Princess Margaret's daughter, Lady Sarah Armstrong-Jones, came out and inspected all the horses. I led the two pale Falabella stallions, Julio Cesar and Carlos, on a walk. I got faint-hearted at the last instant about parading Morenita in her harness with Humphry in the cart – maybe fifteen minutes' practice was not enough after all. So John just led her. My eldest son, Jamie, also helped with the horses. It was a great advantage having him there since he is a towering six-footer who made the Falabellas look even smaller than they are.

I told Sir John about my decision not to bring out the cart, but the Queen's Equerry had taken a great liking to Humphry and insisted that he should join the parade. So he rode on my arm. He showed his gratitude to Sir John Miller by stretching forward in front of the Royal Box and grabbing him by the nose. With his fingers up Sir John's nose, he let out a series of loving noises.

It's rather embarrassing when your monkey does that to someone, especially in full view of the Royal Family. You can't very well just say 'Excuse me' and pull it away as that might be somewhat painful for the victim's nose. So

Sir John and I had to stand close together until Humphry could be persuaded to loosen his grip. It was quite a day.

As the summer wore on, we realised that Kilverstone was finally going to make it. By the end of 1978, more than 160,000 visitors had streamed through the gates that year, many of them old friends who had faithfully returned every season since we had opened the park, many others new-comers who had seen or read about the saga of the Falabellas and the monkeys in our bed. The relief of hard-earned success flowed over me like a warm bath, relief not just for ourselves, not just for all the people who had given of themselves to make the Latin American zoo a reality, but for the animals that had become part of the family. Relief, too, that we would be able to carry on and extend our contribution to protecting the species that have been endangered by man's thoughtlessness and folly.

I felt confident in myself that the magnet that drew people back to Kilverstone was something conveyed by the splendid old lady who came back in the late summer bank holiday weekend, as she had done every season since we opened. 'What makes the difference,' she said, 'is that the animals are happy here.'

How do you tell whether animals are happy? I suppose one test is whether they are reproducing themselves. That summer, Kilverstone was full of the cries and the bustle of young families. There were the jaguars, Jason and Jenny, pawing their cubs. There were the snow geese, sitting on their eggs. There were new babies in the monkey house, new foals in the stables, and five infant capybaras snuffling and rooting in the water meadows. There were the baby bison, clumping along at their parents' heels. And there was Eric, proud paterfamilias of the spider monkey clan, full of affection, reaching out to me and the baby monkeys I carried around. I will never run short of jungle babies.